# Defending a Lawsuit by a Junk Debt Buyer
### (Collection Agency):

# *How a Florida Mom Beat Asset Acceptance, LLC!*

by Sheila R. Muñoz, Ed.D.

# Contents

# First and Foremost

Not every case is identical. Not every case will be won with the same, exact solution(s). Every state has different rules of civil procedure and state collection laws; every court is different. There are many things that will most likely be very similar; however, one's final solutions will be at least somewhat different. The purpose of this book is to describe my journey in detail so that others may glean from it ideas and methods of how they might fight their own battle, as well as have examples they might follow.

Of course, the Federal laws, such as the Fair Debt Collection Practices Act (FDCPA), Fair Credit Reporting Act (FCRA), and Telephone Consumer Protection Act (TCPA), will pertain to everyone. The TCPA is not addressed in this book, as it was not a part of my journey. However, if I had known of its existence at the time, I could have and would have used this law, also. One may benefit from researching this law and using it as it pertains to their case.

Keep in mind that many times arbitration may also be a good option as opposed to using the courtroom to fight a collection lawsuit or potential collection lawsuit, as I did in my case.

Obviously, this author cannot guarantee one can win their case by following exactly what was done here. But many, if not most, who want to or must fight their fight pro se (without legal representation), may find direction and ideas from how I fought my fight pro se and beat Asset Acceptance, LLC! One must look through my case and glean from it what might very well work in their case.

The author of this book is not an attorney. The author has no authorization or training to qualify her to give legal advice. She is not liable for the outcome of one's use of any or all of the information contained in this book. The information in this book is simply an exercise of the author's First Amendment right of free speech and the author's own personal opinions, simply sharing an experience from which others may or may not benefit. In some cases, one may be better served by hiring an attorney.

# Chapter 1

# The Summons, the Complaint, and the Answer with Affirmative Defenses

***Note:*** Asset Acceptance, LLC's, actual Summons and Complaint served on me, along with the attachments, may be found at the end of this chapter. My Answer to their Complaint will be found at the end of Chapter 2.

Our adult daughter is terminally ill and lives with us. She was the only one home when the Process Server came to our door. Our daughter was not feeling well at all that day, and her disease has caused her to not always understand or remember things. Our daughter did not understand what the Process Server was saying when she thrust some papers into our daughter's shaking hands and said the papers were for her mother. The daughter closed the door and laid the papers on the kitchen counter and went back to bed.

When I arrived home that afternoon, I noticed the "Summons" lying on the kitchen counter and asked my daughter what the papers were. Our daughter replied she did not know, only that the papers had been given to her at the door by a woman and was told they were for her mom.

I quickly flipped through the papers, trying to get an idea of what the serious-looking papers were all about. Suddenly I focused on a couple of paragraphs and realized that I was being sued for approximately $14,000 on a credit card account that had been charged off almost four years prior.

The credit card had a $10,000 cap, and when I was forced into stopping making payments on it, it was under that mark. But late fees bumped it over $10,000. Then additional late fees, as well as "over the limit" fees, had swollen the debt to close to $14,000 when it was charged off by the original creditor. With interest and fees continuing to compound and be piled on, the total amount for which I was being sued almost reached the $25,000 mark. My heart began to pound.

How could this be? The debt was "charged off" almost four years ago! I thought that was the end of the debt. I believed it meant that the credit card issuer had "given up" collecting the debt. Out of ignorance, I was so wrong!

I felt guilty not paying the debt, but there had been no choice. When the economy turned south, my business had all but dried up for many months. In the midst of thousands of lay-offs in our county, I still pursued unsuccessfully looking for a job. At the same time, my daughter fell ill and was diagnosed with a terminal illness. She could no longer work, drive, or live on her own, so we had to move her in with us. My husband is on a fixed income and even our mortgage had recently been modified to stave off foreclosure.

I felt defeated. I felt panicked. I was weary of fighting everything in my life. I was just a simple, Florida mom, caring for a terminally ill daughter, and trying to keep our family's lives together.

My mind and heart raced. What was I to do? This was the "straw that broke the camel's back." I had barely been able to keep up with the necessities of life. There was no way I could pay $25,000! I had never even heard of Asset Acceptance, LLC. Who were they?

I reflected back and remembered that for a long while I had received calls from several different collectors, sometimes as many as 20 a day. I did not know that I could have fought back then and could have stopped the calls! Naively, I chose to avoid them.

I had refused to answer calls outside of my area code or those marked "Private" or "Unknown." After two or three years of this, the calls had dwindled down to an occasional one now and then, maybe only three or four in a week. I had mistakenly thought I was slowly being forgotten.

Suddenly reality sunk in. One creditor had not forgotten! What was I to do? I had never been a defendant in any kind of court case before; I had never even received a traffic ticket! I did not know where to turn. Should I ignore the Summons and whatever "'twill be, 'twill be"? I thought seriously of tossing the paperwork into the trash. Later, I learned that would have been a HUGE mistake!

# Junk Debt Buyers (JDBs) Use Fear, Humiliation, and Intimidation

The first step in taking charge of a similar situation is DON'T PANIC! Fear is one's worst enemy. Collection agencies' tactics include fear, intimidation, and humiliation. These emotions are extremely uncomfortable, and most people will avoid them at almost any cost. Debt collectors, especially Junk Debt Buyers (JDBs), know only too well that many people will succumb to these tactics. But with knowledge, one can fight and, very possibly, win!

To win, one must put their pride and emotions aside. If I allowed pride to come in, this book would not be written. Emotions will only cloud one's judgment. Fear, feelings of worthlessness, guilt, and shame all need to be looked at for what they are and then set aside. They have no place in a fight such as this.

As Benjamin Mee said in the movie, *We Bought a Zoo,* "You know, sometimes all you need is 20 seconds of insane courage. Just literally 20 seconds of just embarrassing bravery. And I promise you, something great will come of it." That is the main requirement to win!

This Florida mom did not know how to hire an attorney. Could I even afford an attorney? Our family had used up all our savings and retirement plan monies trying to tread water financially through the downturn in the economy and our daughter's illness.

Suddenly, I remembered we held a membership in a prepaid legal plan. Hope began to dawn for me. The next morning I called the prepaid legal firm that was associated with our membership. The attorney asked me if the debt was mine. I answered that it could very possibly be mine, but after looking more carefully at the Complaint Asset Acceptance, LLC, served, it held nothing that proved to me the specific account over which they were suing me was, without doubt, mine. There was nothing to prove the amount for which they were suing was accurate.

My identity had been stolen twice in the last 10 years. Could this be fallout from that? I no longer had the credit card or any statements for the account in question. It looked as though there was a possibility the account was mine, but there was absolutely no way I could 100% verify it by the paperwork provided by Asset Acceptance, LLC, in the Summons and Complaint.

The attorney on the phone gruffly said, "Well, you need to answer the Summons and Complaint within 20 calendar days. In the meantime, I will refer you to a bankruptcy attorney in your area. Take your paperwork to them and let them decide if you should file bankruptcy or if there is an alternative. From what you tell me, it sounds like you either need to pay the debt or file bankruptcy." He then gave me the name and phone number of an attorney not far from our home.

I was further disheartened, and fear started creeping back in. I did not want to file bankruptcy, except as a last resort. Heck, I did not even have the money to file bankruptcy! I had fought off bankruptcy for the last three or four years and believed the battle was almost over. My credit score had already gone from the high 700s to low 800s four years before to under 600 at the moment. A bankruptcy would be on my credit report 10 years after it was discharged! That was like starting all over again in repairing my creditworthiness.

Also, how was I to answer the Summons and Complaint? I knew nothing as to how that should be accomplished. I had no legal training. Again, I even thought of just giving up and throwing away the Summons and Complaint.

But after giving more thought to it, I was not ready to give up just yet! I called the attorney to whom I was referred and made an appointment a couple of days away. Twenty days started ticking away quickly!

When my husband and I arrived at the law firm, the attorney bluntly told us that he did not deal with bankruptcy or debt issues very much at all, but he would look over the paperwork. After a few minutes of silence while the attorney perused the Summons and Complaint, he said, "Normally, I charge $1,500 for bankruptcy. Since you are a member of a prepaid legal plan, I will charge you $1,200. It must be paid before the bankruptcy is filed. If you don't have the $1,200 now or within a few days, you must answer the Summons. You only have 20 days to answer the Summons or a default judgment will be entered against you, and a week has already passed. If you want me to answer the Summons for you, that will be an additional fee. What would you like to do?"

I looked at my husband, and he looked questioningly back at me. I spoke up, "But by these papers, who can say if this debt is mine? What if it's not? Besides, we don't have $1,200 to file for bankruptcy nor money to pay you to answer the Summons for us."

The attorney said, "Well, you can answer the Summons yourself, then."

I asked, "How do I do that?"

He said, "Follow the same format as the Complaint, and answer each and every numbered paragraph with either 'Admit' or 'Deny.' Then, if you decide you want to file bankruptcy, as soon as you get the $1,200, you can come back and see me."

Another blow. Wow! Should I give up and just let the court place a default judgment on me? The attorney explained a default judgment would mean the court would order me to pay the debt. If I could not pay it, a lien could be placed against our home and could stay on our home and on my credit report for up to 20 years! I was self-employed, but if I was working an outside job, my wages would be garnished. My bank account would be frozen or garnished. If I had had any savings, those could have been confiscated, as well. Depending on the state, even retirement savings and much more can be affected.

"But did I have grounds on which to fight?" I wondered. Could I win if I fought? One thing for sure: I could not afford to file bankruptcy. Nor could I afford to pay the debt, even if Asset Acceptance, LLC, agreed to settle for a smaller amount. I could not afford to hire an attorney, if I could even find one willing to help. Was this debt even mine? I did not know the answers, but I was certainly determined to find them!

For the next 36 hours, I barely slept or ate. Time was running out. I researched all over the internet, simply looking for answers as to how to answer a summons and what a judgment would mean if I chose not to answer and fight. In the end, what I accumulated in knowledge and confidence to fight my case pro se ended up amounting to well over 1,000 hours of research and study.

The purpose of this book is, hopefully, to help others cut through the chase and get to the meat of the items that may help them fight their own personal war with a junk debt buyer. One would not use every item in this book, as their case will be different. Many cases end up being much simpler than this one and more easily settled. However, there are usually many similarities in JDB lawsuits. One may sort through what I did and pick and choose items that may fit their particular situation. At the very least, the first step is to answer the Summons and Complaint if one is sued.

If this is where the reader finds himself, this author is certain that the reader will find gems herein that will either help the reader by face value or point the reader in the direction of where to look for further information.

## Definitions and Explanations

Let's lay out a foundation. There are some preliminary things one must understand before commencing the battle. Some important definitions are:

### 1. Junk Debt Buyer (JDB) vs. Original Creditor

This book is geared to those fighting a lawsuit by a Junk Debt Buyer (JDB) or collection agency as opposed to an original creditor. An original creditor is the company or bank with which one acquires the credit card or debt in the first place. Fighting a lawsuit by the original creditor would follow a different path than what is portrayed in this book, as certain laws only pertain to JDBs or collection agencies as opposed to original creditors.

Most delinquent debt is charged off the creditor's books after six months of delinquency. However, the original creditor may still attempt to collect the debt through phone calls and/or dunning letters. Just because a debt is charged off does not mean debt collection attempts will cease. More typically, the original creditor will either assign or sell the debt to a JDB.

When a charged off debt is **assigned** to a JDB, the original creditor maintains ownership of the debt, but simply assigns a JDB to collect on the debt for them. Basically, the original creditor farms out the collection of a debt to a JDB in exchange for a share in the profit of any amounts collected.

If an assigned JDB is unsuccessful in collecting the debt, the debt goes back to the original creditor. The original creditor may again attempt to collect the debt, or they may choose to farm it out again, this time to a different JDB, to try their hand at collecting the debt.

When a charged off debt is **sold** to a JDB, the JDB buys a portfolio of debt. The original creditor no longer owns the debt and usually no longer has any financial interest in the debt. This purchased portfolio contains many charged off accounts that can be in the millions. JDBs typically pay an average of 3% for the debt, sometimes less. In other words, they pay three cents on the dollar for the debt. If one has a charged off debt of $1,000, the JDB may only pay $30 or less for that debt. The JDB then attempts to collect the debt from the consumer themselves.

That is why JDBs many times offer a one-time settlement of 25% off or 30% off if the consumer pays the debt in a lump sum. The JDB is still making a profit on the debt. In the $1,000 debt example above, as long as they make over $30 on the debt, they have profited. So, the JDB may offer a consumer to pay $750 or $700 instead of the full $1,000. Nice profit, huh?

It is this author's opinion that if she had had a lump sum of money to settle with Asset Acceptance, LLC, or with any JDB, she would offer to settle for only 10% of the original debt. In the above example, she would only offer to pay $100 to settle the debt in full, nothing more.

If one chooses this route, he must be careful settlement is given in writing that the debt is paid in full by the lump sum payment and the remaining portion is deleted. Otherwise, the remainder of the debt could be sold to another JDB or given back to the original creditor for them to try to collect on the remainder. And the cycle starts all over again, while the consumer thought the debt was settled.

Once a JDB is assigned or sold a debt, the phone calls typically start. By law (Fair Debt Collection Practices Act – FDCPA), a JDB can only call between 8a and 9p. They can call a consumer on Sunday; they can call a consumer on Thanksgiving; they can even call the consumer on Christmas. They can call any day, as long as it is between the hours of 8a and 9p.

One may write the JDB a letter stating that all phone calls are inconvenient and that they must communicate with them only in writing. The JDB must honor that request. If not, they are violating federal law and could set themselves up to being sued by the consumer. However, it has been assumed that this can also sometimes trigger the filing of a lawsuit against the consumer by the JDB, especially if the debt is still within the statute of limitations (more on that later). But, in the least, it should stop the phone calls.

As already stated, the JDB's set of tools are mostly fear, intimidation, and humiliation. Most people will buckle under it because they are uninformed, and their pride gets in the way. JDBs know this. The collector on the phone may swear, raise their voice, make one feel like the lowest scum, etc., all of which are illegal for them to do. They may threaten to confiscate property, also illegal to do.

It may be best to refuse to speak to them. Problems can arise if one inadvertently admits the debt or if one says they will pay the debt or make a partial payment at some later time. The consumer may ask for a mailing address, hinting it is needed to send a payment. Once the mailing address is obtained, the consumer can mail a letter that "all calls are inconvenient." This should stop the phone calls from that JDB. I only wish I had known that when I was receiving 20 to 30 calls a day!

## 2. Statute of Limitations and Time-Barred Debt

The statute of limitations on filing a lawsuit in an attempt to collect a debt varies state by state. One must research on the internet for the statute of limitations for their state.

When one is sued over a debt, there are actually two statutes of limitations that should be referenced. One is the statue of limitations for the state in which the consumer resides and one is the statute of limitations of the state where the original creditor's corporation is headquartered. If the state in which the consumer resides has a longer statute of limitations than the state of the original creditor, many states will "borrow" the statute of the state with the shorter time limit to the benefit of the consumer. The act of "borrowing" a statute varies by state.

The statute of limitations also depends, in many states, on what type of debt it is. In the case portrayed in this book, it is an alleged credit card debt by a Florida family. In Florida, the statute of limitations for filing a lawsuit on a credit card debt is four years. The four years commences from the first month of delinquency, the first payment that was missed. Debt created by a written contract (auto loan, mortgage, etc.) has a longer statute of limitations.

In the case portrayed in this book, the Complaint states that the last payment on the credit card debt was on or about 4/2007. That would make the statute of limitations by Florida law to end 4/2011. The lawsuit was filed 3/2011, one month prior to the statute of limitations' ending.

Here is where a question arises in my mind. Asset Acceptance, LLC, proclaims that I made my last payment on a credit card debt on or about 4/2007. However, no statements or paperwork of any kind was attached to their Complaint. They filed their lawsuit one month prior to the statute of limitations running out if my last payment was, in fact, 4/2007. But what if Asset Acceptance, LLC, was not truthful, and my last payment was actually 3/2007 or 2/2007?

If the statute of limitations for the state of the original creditor is shorter than the four years, in some states, the court may uphold the statute of limitations of the state of the original creditor (borrow the statute). This can be a powerful tool to get a lawsuit dismissed "with prejudice" in many cases on the basis that the debt is "time-barred." ("With prejudice" and "Without prejudice" will be discussed later in this book.)

A "time-barred" debt means too much time has passed for a creditor or JDB to sue you over the debt. The original creditor or JDB can still attempt to collect on the debt. Even when a JDB knows the debt is outside the statute of limitations, they may still make the phone calls and send the letters in an attempt to collect on the debt. It is actually common for them to still move ahead and file a lawsuit, hoping the consumer is uninformed on statute of limitation issues. If the consumer is uninformed and does not answer the Summons and Complaint or claim in their Answer to the Summons and Complaint that the debt is time barred, the consumer may have a default judgment placed on them when it could have easily been avoided.

The statute of limitations can be suspended and reset, oftentimes without the consumer realizing it. When a lawsuit is filed, the running of the statute of limitations is suspended or "tolled." An example could be that there are four weeks left on the statute of limitations during which a JDB could file a lawsuit. They file. The remaining four weeks are put on hold, tolled. If the case is dismissed with or without prejudice voluntarily by the JDB, the statute of limitations is unaffected. It would be as if the lawsuit had never been filed. The statute of limitations would have continued running right through the lawsuit and ended four weeks after the lawsuit was filed.

However, if the case continues until there is a partial settlement or is resolved in any other way, the statute of limitations will pick back up at the close of the case from where it left off when the lawsuit was initially filed. For example, if a partial settlement is reached and the settlement does not stipulate that the remainder of the debt is extinguished, the JDB could sell the remainder of the debt to another JDB, and the new JDB has four weeks in which they could file a lawsuit on the leftover debt.

Another way the statute of limitations could be reset or extended is by the words of the consumer. That is why it is usually best to not even talk to a debt collector. If a consumer should promise they will pay sometime in the future, or if they make a partial payment, no matter how small, the statute of limitations for that state is reset from that date. It completely starts over.

One more thing I learned I needed to pay attention to: Let's say a consumer has more than one debt in default. Maybe he has three credit cards in default. The consumer receives a lump sum of money, such as a tax return or a bonus at work. He decides to pay a substantial amount on one of the debts to get that one debt out of his hair. The FDCPA rules that the money would need to be divided up among the default debts, not all paid to one. And oh, by the way, paying any portion of it resets the statute of limitations on each debt!

The statute of limitations to file a lawsuit on an alleged debt is not the same for the statute of limitations for a charged off debt to remain on a credit report. That is seven years from the date of the charge-off, which is 180 days after the debt becomes delinquent (total of 7½ years from the first missed payment).

Although in Florida the statute of limitations during which a JDB may file a lawsuit in an attempt to collect a debt is four years, a JDB may continue to attempt to collect (dunning letters, collection calls, etc.) on the debt as long as the debt remains unpaid. They simply cannot use the legal system in order to do so once the statute of limitations has expired. Here is where a letter telling the JDB all calls are inconvenient can really help.

A consumer would be wise to be well versed in the FDCPA and TCPA to help stop nuisance collection calls and letters, especially after the statute of limitations has ended. There are resources and forums on the internet that may be extremely helpful in these situations.

## 3. Default Judgment

In answering a Summons, every state has its own timeframe in which the Summons must be answered. The Summons itself will state the amount of time one has to answer the Summons. In Florida, it is 20 calendar days unless the 20th day falls on the weekend or a holiday. Then it is the first day after the weekend or holiday.

To ignore or refuse to answer the Summons allows the JDB to Motion for a Default Summary Judgment. **<u>Approximately 90% of those who are served with a Summons and a Complaint by a JDB never answer the Summons</u>**. They are fearful and do not know what to do. Some believe if they ignore it, it will simply go away. JDBs make their money on the many default judgments awarded to them every year on persons who never even answer the lawsuit. According to their website, Asset Acceptance, LLC, makes approximately $250 million a year in collections!

The truth is, it will NOT go away!  A Default Summary Judgment in Florida can be signed by the Clerk of Court. It does not even have to go before a judge. It basically means the Defendant (the consumer) has not denied any of the accusations by the JDB; therefore, the Complaint must be true. Therefore, the Clerk of Court may sign the Default Judgment.

Unless one is judgment proof (explained later in this chapter) at the time and informs the court of their status, this is the time when wages may be garnished, bank accounts may be frozen, assets may be taken in order to satisfy the debt. Even if one is judgment proof, it does not mean they will remain judgment proof forever. The JDB is patient to wait until the time if and when a consumer on which a judgment has been placed is no longer judgment proof.

Again, each state has its own timeframe, but in Florida, a judgment remains on a consumer for 10 years and can be renewed by the JDB at the end of the 10 years for another 10 years, for a total of 20 years. If a judgment-proof consumer is no longer judgment proof any time during those 20 years, the JDB can go after their assets. Of course, during all this time, the judgment remains on the credit report, also, having a drastic effect on the credit score. It can affect employment possibilities, as well.

## 4. The Laws Involved

The major laws that govern a JDB's debt collection actions are the Fair Debt Collection Practices Act (FDCPA), the Fair Credit Reporting Act (FCRA), the Telephone Consumer Protection Act (TCPA), the Rules of Civil Procedure for one's state (or Federal Rules of Civil Procedure for Federal court), and state consumer laws regarding debt collection. In Florida, it is the Fair Credit Collection Practices Act (FCCPA) that closely mirrors the FDCPA. The FDCPA, TCPA, and FCRA are Federal laws.

The FDCPA allows for declaratory judgment, actual/statutory damages, and reasonable attorney's fees and costs. If one is fighting a lawsuit pro se, they typically do not qualify for attorney's fees and costs. However, a Defendant (consumer) may find it wise to add it into a counterclaim, because, if at any time the Defendant would find the need to bring in an attorney to help, that attorney's fees and costs may be covered if the counterclaim was granted by the court. In other words, one could put it into a counterclaim in case it was needed.

The FDCPA allows for $100-$1,000 in statutory (by law) damages total. The violations are not "stackable." That means it is not per violation, simply $100-$1,000 in total damages, no matter if there is one violation or 10 violations.

The FDCPA is a strict liability statute, meaning one violation is sufficient to establish liability. There can be many violations. One would be wise to take the time to read through the FDCPA carefully, making notes of the JDB's non-compliance. Again, every case is different, so every case would yield different possible violations.

The FCRA allows for $100-$1,000 in statutory (by law) damages for EACH violation. In other words, the violations are "stackable." In addition, another $1,000 may be added for each non-permissible pull (Section 604 of the FCRA) of one's credit report, if applicable. If a non-permissible pull was performed from all three credit reporting agencies, this would be three violations up to $1,000 each.

If a JDB pulls a credit report under false pretenses, such as stating it is for a credit card account, when the debt is no longer a credit card account, the penalty can be up to two years in prison for the violator. Once a JDB is sold an account, it becomes a "debt buyer account," no longer a credit card account.

It is important to note the FCRA also allows for punitive damages and attorneys' fees and costs. Once again, one would be prudent to take the time to carefully read through the FCRA. In certain cases, punitive damages can be substantial.

Then there are the state laws and the state's or Federal Rules of Civil Procedure. Both must be carefully read to find possible violations by the JDB, as well as to discover monetary damages (if any) that are available to the consumer. Violations by the JDB of the Rules of Civil Procedure may only yield a dismissal of a case with or without prejudice, but that is winning the case! A win is a win!

## 5. Being Judgment Proof

Being judgment proof varies by state, as well. In my case, I was judgment proof by Florida law:

- I was Head of Household (I had a child living with me for whom I provided at least 50% of her support).

- My husband was on Social Security Disability, and we only had one bank account.

- The money in the bank account included a mingling of Social Security Disability funds, which cannot be touched by a judgment.

- I live in a home that is homesteaded and own no other real estate. A homesteaded home in Florida is exempt from a judgment.

- I no longer had any retirement or other assets.

- I was self-employed and had no garnishable wages.

- I had no equity in any vehicles.

- I had no other assets.

Of course, a judgment-proof consumer's situation may very well change in the course of the years during which a judgment remains, such as the 20 years in Florida. Once a Defendant loses judgment-proof status, they are fair game to the JDB to go after payment on the judgment.

## 6. With Prejudice or Without Prejudice

When a lawsuit or motion is dismissed by a court, it is either dismissed "with prejudice" or "without prejudice." Usually, one would consider "without" prejudice to be better.

However, in court, "without prejudice" allows the losing entity to correct any mistakes or deficiencies and then come back and refile the lawsuit. Or, in the case of a motion dismissed by a judge without prejudice, it allows the entity to fix something the motion addresses in order to get back on track with the lawsuit.

"With prejudice" means it is the end of that lawsuit or motion. If a case is dismissed with prejudice, the one doing the suing cannot come back at a later time and sue again. It is done, finished. In the case of a motion, if it is dismissed with prejudice by a judge, the party cannot fix something and come back with it. That motion is defeated and is dead.

If a case is voluntarily dismissed by the JDB, with or without prejudice, the statute of limitations is considered to continue to run as if a lawsuit had never been filed. If the statute of limitations should run out while the lawsuit is running, as it did with my case, and the case is voluntarily dismissed by the JDB, the lawsuit is, in effect, dismissed with prejudice, as a lawsuit can never be filed by anyone on that debt. It is now outside the statute of limitations.

In the case of a JDB filing a lawsuit against a consumer, the desired conclusion for that lawsuit for the consumer is a dismissal with prejudice by the JDB or by the judge. That JDB cannot come back and sue again for that same debt at a later time. However, if the statute of limitations still has time on it, the debt may be sold to another JDB, and that JDB may file suit to attempt to collect the debt. The consumer would then have to lather, rinse, and repeat.

## Answering the Summons

The MOST IMPORTANT thing one can do once they have been served with a Summons and a Complaint is to **ANSWER IT**! One should be very sure of the timeframe within which they have to work.

The MOST IMPORTANT thing one can do BEFORE answering the Summons and Complaint is to become very familiar with their state's Rules of Civil Procedure. This is another area where states are diverse. The internet will yield one's state's Rules of Civil Procedure or the Federal Rules of Civil Procedure, whichever applies.

Did this author say "become very familiar with their state's Rules of Civil Procedure"? Yes! It is so very important. Pull up a chair and read them thoroughly. There may be sections that do not pertain to one's particular lawsuit, but much of it will. Become VERY FAMILIAR with them! It is the instruction manual! Read them slowly and carefully. The court will demand following them.

Some states allow one to file a Motion To Dismiss in lieu of an answer. This information would be found in the state's Rules of Civil Procedure. It is not an option in Florida.

In Florida, the Answer to the Summons and Complaint should include the Answer, Affirmative Defenses, and a Counterclaim, if needed. In my case, I answered the Summons and Complaint and provided Affirmative Defenses. From lack of information, I erroneously did not file a counterclaim at this point, but this will be discussed later in the book.

At this point, it should also be pointed out that Arbitration may be provided for in a credit card agreement. Many credit card companies are deleting this out of their card agreements, as it is very costly to the original creditor or JDBs when consumers choose to fight in this arena. This book does not explore the option of Arbitration, although it is a viable sword for some to use. It may be an option one would want to research further. Some internet forums deliver great information on this issue.

However, if one prefers to use Arbitration, states differ on when the court needs to be made aware of the choice of that option. It usually is very early in defending oneself in a lawsuit by a JDB. In some states, if Arbitration is chosen, the Summons and Complaint is not answered. In those states, answering the Complaint may cancel the Arbitration option. It is wise to research this option early before answering the Summons and Complaint and advise the court accordingly.

In my case, I answered the Complaint very simply and offered Affirmative Defenses. Basically, I denied everything other than my name and address (which the JDB already had), as the JDB had offered no proof that would enable me to admit unequivocally to the charges.

Pointing to the second point of the Complaint regarding whether the JDB has authority to do business in the state in which the consumer resides, it is important for the consumer to check on licensure of the JDB to do business in the state in which the consumer resides. It would be a mistake to assume that since the JDB filed a lawsuit that they would have a current license in that particular state. If the JDB is not licensed, that would be an affirmative defense. In Florida, a collection agency must have a license and pay a bond. Whether a JDB is licensed in Florida may be found on the website for Florida Office of Financial Regulation.

At the time I filed my Answer and Affirmative Defenses, I believed I did not have anything to really counterclaim. A Counterclaim is actually a lawsuit against the JDB for their violations. However, after I had already filed my Answer to the Summons and Complaint and Affirmative Defenses, I continued to research. Especially after Discovery, I found I had much to include in a Counterclaim. Unfortunately, I failed to ask leave (permission) of the court to file a Counterclaim, which is stipulated in the Florida Rules of Civil Procedure. You see, I did not follow the rules! This will be covered more in a later chapter.

If there are issues with which one may counterclaim, the Florida Rules of Civil Procedure allow for the Counterclaim to be added to the Answer to the Summons and Complaint after the Affirmative Defenses. Otherwise the consumer must ask leave of the court before filing a Counterclaim. This would be done in the form of a motion.

At the end of the Answer and Affirmative Defenses (and Counterclaim, if applicable), there needs to be a Certificate of Service. Actually, with each and every document filed with the court, a Certificate of Service must be attached. Courts may vary on how this may look. One may check other court cases filed at the courthouse or may possibly be able to ask the office of the Clerk of Court. I simply tried to format my documents to match those that were sent to me by the JDB.

Once the Summons and Complaint have been answered, three copies need to be made. One copy is for the consumer's own records; one is to be filed with the Clerk of Court; one is mailed to the attorney who issued the Summons and Complaint. This should be sent certified mail, return receipt requested (CMRRR), as proof that the JDB received it. Sometimes the JDB will say otherwise, and proof will be needed.

My Answer to Asset Acceptance, LLC's, Summons and Complaint will be found at the end of Chapter 2, after their "evidence" attached to their Complaint has been explained and dissected.

# The Actual Summons and Complaint from Asset Acceptance, LLC, with Attached "Evidence"

IN THE COUNTY COURT,
IN AND FOR POLK COUNTY, FLORIDA
CIVIL DIVISION

ASSET ACCEPTANCE, LLC
    Plaintiff,

vs.                              Case No.

SHEILA R MUNOZ             53-20?? CC-00 19?5
    Defendant.
_____/

SUMMONS
PERSONAL SERVICE ON A NATURAL PERSON

TO:   SHEILA R MUNOZ

IMPORTANT

    A lawsuit has been filed against you. You have 20 calendar days after this summons is served on you to file a written response to the attached complaint with the clerk of this court. A phone call will not protect you. Your written response, including the case number given above and the names of the parties, must be filed if you want the court to hear your side of the case. If you do not file your response on time, you may lose the case, and your wages, money, and property may thereafter be taken without further warning from the court. There are other legal requirements. You may want to call an attorney right away. If you do not know an attorney, you may call an attorney referral service or a legal aid office (listed in the phone book).

    If you choose to file a written response yourself, at the same time you file your written response to the court, you must also mail or take a copy of your written response to the "Plaintiff/Plaintiff's Attorney" named below.

IMPORTANTE

    USTED HA SIDO DEMANDADO LEGALMENTE. TIENE 20 DIAS, CONTADOS A PARTIR DEL RECIBO DE ESTA NOTIFICACION, PARA CONTESTAR LA DEMANDA ADJUNTA, POR ESCRITO, Y PRESENTARLA ANTE ESTE TRIBUNAL. UNA LLAMADA TELEFONICA NO LO PROTEGERA. SI USTED DESEA QUE EL TRIBUNAL CONSIDERE SU DEFENSA, DEBE PRESENTAR SU RESPUESTA POR ESCRITO, INCLUYENDO EL NUMERO DEL CASO Y LOS NOMBRES DE LAS PARTES INTERESADAS. SI USTED NO CONTESTA LA DEMANDA A TIEMPO, PUDIESE PERDER EL CASO Y PODRIA SER DESPOJADO DE SUS INGRESO Y PROPIEDADES, O PRIVADO DE SUS DERECHOS, SIN PREVIO AVISO DEL TRIBUNAL. EXISTEN O TROS REQUISITO LEGALES. SI LO DESEA, PUEDE USTED CONSULTAR A UN ABOGADO IMMEDIATEMENTE. SI NO CONOCE A UN ABOGADO, PUEDE LLAMAR A UNA DE

FL_6\00G Account No: 10-450001837

METE NUMERO KA-A KI SOU TET PAGELA AVEC NOM MOUNE-YO KI SOU PAPIE-SA OBLIGE ECRI SI OU VLE KE TRIBUNAL-LA TENDE POSITION-OU COU KA-A. SI OU PA ENREGISTRE RESPONSE-OU A L'HEURE OU CAPAB PEDU KA-A SAN TRIBUNAL LA PA ANNOUNCE-OU EN YEN, OU CAPAB PEDU L'AGEN OU AK BYEN OU. GENYEN LOT DEMANDE. OU KA BESOIN TELEPHONE YON AVOKE TOUT DE SUIT. SI OU PA LONEN YON AVOKE, OU KA RELE SEVIS KI REKOMANDE AVOKA. OU BIRO EDE LEGAL (KIN AN LIS LIV TELEPHONE).

SI OU SHOISI VOYE YON REPONCE PA ECRI OUMENM, OU SUPPOSE EN MEM TAN POSTE EN MEM TAN POSTE ON POTE ON COPI RESPONSE PA ECRI POU AVOKA PLEYAN OU PLENAN-YO KE NON-LI AMA-A ET ENREGISTRE REPONCE-LA NAN TRIBUNAL-LA KI LOCALIZE NAN AVEK SEKRETE TRIBINAL. ADRES SANTRAL BIWO SEKRETE A SE DADA COUNTY COURTHOUSE. ADRES TRIBUNAL LA. AK ADRES LOT TRIBUNAL YON AN LIS KI ANBA A POU OU KA JWENN YO ALEZ:

RODOLFO J. MIRO, ANTHONY J. STEELE. AMANDA DUFFY OR HOWARD BUTLER. IN HOUSE COUNSELS FOR:

ASSET ACCEPTANCE, LLC
2840 S. Faulkenburg Road
Riverview FL 33569
(866) 266-7660 OR (813) 569-0400


THE STATE OF FLORIDA
To Each Sheriff of the State:

YOU ARE COMMANDED to serve this summons and a copy of the complaint in this lawsuit on the above-named defendant.

DATED on: _____MAR 3 1 2011___, 2011.

                                              By:_____
                                                   /s/ Wendy Anoni
                                              Deputy Clerk

(SEAL)

ASSET ACCEPTANCE, LLC
      Plaintiff.

vs.                                Case No.

SHEILA R MUNOZ
      Defendant(s).
_____/

## COMPLAINT

COMES NOW, the Plaintiff, ASSET ACCEPTANCE, LLC, sues Defendant(s), SHEILA R MUNOZ, and alleges:

1. Damages in this action exceed $5000 but not $15,000 exclusive of interests and court costs.

2. Plaintiff, ASSET ACCEPTANCE, LLC, is a Delaware Limited Liability Company authorized and doing business in the State of Florida.

3. Plaintiff is informed and believes that the Defendant(s), SHEILA R MUNOZ is/are a resident of POLK County, Florida.

4. On or about November 26, 2004 to on or about April 30, 2007 Defendant(s) caused charges to be incurred on their Citibank credit card account numbered ███████████. Defendant made a partial payment on or about April 30, 2007.

5. ASSET ACCEPTANCE, LLC purchased, for value, the Defendant's CITIBANK credit card account, thereby creating a right in favor of ASSET ACCEPTANCE, LLC, and against Defendant.

6. All conditions precedent to the bringing of this action have occurred, been performed or have been waived.

## COUNT 1 - BREACH OF CONTRACT

7. Plaintiff repeats and re-alleges each and every material allegation as contained in paragraphs 1 through 6 above.

8. Prior to institution of this action, the Defendant applied to CITIBANK for a credit card.

9. Pursuant to a written agreement between the parties, CITIBANK established a credit card account in the name of the Defendant(s) and issued a CITIBANK card, bearing the number ███████████.

10. The CITIBANK card, and the original of the Agreement, were mailed to the

FI_0115 Account No : 10-800901837

Defendant(s).

11. The Defendant, after receiving the CITIBANK card, together with the Agreement, used the account and card by making charges thereon. Upon information and belief, Plaintiff alleges that the Defendant also signed the card, which is or was in the Defendant's possession and/or control. Subsequent charges or payments ratified and re-affirms the terms and conditions of the agreement and the current outstanding balance and is a promise to pay the same. By making charges on the account, the Defendant accepted the terms of the Agreement and a contract was entered into between Plaintiff and Defendant.

12. Charges were incurred on the account in the sum of $13,171.06. The Defendant breached the Agreement by failing to make the payment due on the account.

13. The Defendant(s) is to notify the credit card issuer of any objections or errors on the periodic statements in writing within 60 days of the rendition of any statement.

14. The Defendant has made no objection to the statements to the credit card issuer.

15. The Defendant's use of the card and making payments on the account ratifies the present outstanding balance, and is a promise to pay the same.

16. There is now due and owing by reason of the breach of the Agreement the principal sum of $13,171.06, together with interest in the amount of $10,253.94.

17. Demand has been made for the sums due and owing but Defendant has failed and refused, and continues to fail and refuse to pay this amount.

18. As a result of Defendant's actions, Plaintiff has been damaged in the amount of $13,171.06, plus interest of $10,253.94.

WHEREFORE, Plaintiff demands judgment against Defendant(s) SHEILA R. MUNOZ, in the amount of $13,171.06 plus pre-judgment accrued interest in the amount of $10,253.94 through March 03, 2011 and continuing plus the cost of this action.

## COUNT II - ACCOUNT STATED

19. Plaintiff re-alleges the allegations set forth in paragraphs 1 through 6 of the Complaint as if fully set forth herein.

20. Before the institution of this action, CITIBANK and Defendant(s) had business transactions between them, and they agreed to the resulting balance.

21. CITIBANK rendered a statement to the Defendant(s) and Defendant(s) did not object to the statement.

22. The Defendant(s) is indebted to CITIBANK and by virtue of an agreement, Plaintiff, for the principal sum of $13,171.06, that is due with interest in the amount of $10,253.94 on the account.

WHEREFORE, Plaintiff demands judgment against Defendant(s) SHEILA R. MUNOZ, in the amount of $13,171.06 plus pre-judgment accrued interest in the amount of $10,253.94

through March 03, 2011 and continuing plus the cost of this action. /S/ Amanda R. Duffy

( ) Rodolfo J. Miro, Bar No. 0103799
( ) Anthony J. Steele, Bar No. 0074810
( ) Howard Butler, Bar No. 0753041
( ) Amanda Duffy, Bar No. 0035612
Staff Attorney for Plaintiff
ASSET ACCEPTANCE, LLC
PO BOX 9065
BRANDON FL 33509
(866) 266-7660
(813) 983 2519 facsimile

THIS COMMUNICATION IS FROM A DEBT COLLECTOR

## BILL OF SALE AND ASSIGNMENT

THIS BILL OF SALE AND ASSIGNMENT is dated June 30, 2010, between Citibank (South Dakota), N.A., a national banking association organized under the laws of the United States, located at 701 East 60th Street North, Sioux Falls, SD 57117 (the "Bank") and Asset Acceptance, LLC ("Buyer"), organized under the laws of the Delaware, with its headquarters/principal place of business at 28405 Van Dyke Ave, Warren, MI 48093.

For value received and subject to the terms and conditions of the Purchase and Sale Agreement dated June 29, 2010, between Buyer and the Bank (the "Agreement"), the Bank does hereby transfer, sell, assign, convey, grant, bargain, set over and deliver to Buyer, and to Buyer's successors and assigns, the Accounts listed in Exhibit 1 and the final electronic file.

Citibank (South Dakota), N.A.                      Asset Acceptance, LLC

By: _____                      By: _____
          (Signature)                                       (Signature)

Name: Douglas C. Morrison                          Name: _____

Title: Vice President & CFO                        Title: SVP & Chief Acquisitions Officer

# CARD AGREEMENT

This Card Agreement, which includes your card carrier, is your contract with us and governs the use of your card and account. The card carrier contains important account information, including your annual percentage rates and the amount of any membership fee. Please read and keep these documents for your records.

### FACTS ABOUT RATES AND FEES

For complete information about these facts, please see the related sections in this Card Agreement.

## RATES—FINANCE CHARGES

**Purchase and Cash Advance APRs:** See card carrier. All APRs based on the Prime Rate may vary each billing period.

**Default APR:** See card carrier. The Default APR equals the Prime Rate plus up to 23.99%, or up to 32.99%, whichever is greater. All APRs may automatically increase up to the Default APR if you fail to make a payment to us when due, exceed your credit line, or make a payment to us that is not honored.

**Minimum Finance Charge:** $0.50

## TRANSACTION FEES—FINANCE CHARGES

**Balance Transfer Fee:** 3% of each balance transfer ($5 minimum; $75 maximum)

**Purchases Made in a Foreign Currency Fee:** 3% of each purchase after its conversion into U.S. dollars

**Cash Advance Fee:** 3% of each cash advance, $5 minimum

## OTHER FEES

**Late Fee:** $15 on balances up to $100; $29 on balances of $100.01 to $250; $39 on balances of $250 and over

**Over-the-Credit-Line Fee:** $29

**Annual Membership Fee:** See card carrier

**Returned Payment Fee:** $39

**Returned Convenience Check Fee:** $39

**Stop Payment on Convenience Check Fee:** $39

**Rates, fees, and terms may change:** We may change the rates, fees, and terms of your account at any time for any reason. These reasons may be based on information in your credit report, such as your failure to make payments to another creditor when due, amounts owed to other creditors, the number of credit accounts outstanding, or the number of credit inquiries. These reasons may also include competitive or market related factors. If we make a change for any of those reasons, you will receive advance notice and a right to opt out in accordance with applicable law.

## Definitions

**account:** the relationship established between you and us by this Card Agreement.

**APR:** annual percentage rate.

**authorized user:** any person you allow to use your account.

**card:** one or more cards or other account access devices, including account numbers, that we issue to you to obtain credit under this Card Agreement.

**Card Agreement (or Agreement):** this document and the card carrier.

**we, us, and our:** Citibank (South Dakota), N.A., the issuer of your account.

**you, your, and yours:** the person who applied to open the account and any other person responsible for complying with this Agreement, including the person to whom we address billing statements.

## Your Account

You agree to use your account in accordance with this Agreement. This Agreement is binding on you unless you cancel your account within 30 days after receiving the card and you have not used or authorized use of the card. You must pay us for all amounts due on your account as specified in this Agreement. Your account must only be used for lawful transactions.

**Authorized Users:** You may allow authorized users to use your account. You may request additional cards for authorized users. You must pay us for all charges made by authorized users even if you did not intend to be responsible for those charges. You must notify us to revoke any permission you give to an authorized user to use a card or to use your account.

**Credit Line:** Your initial credit line appears on the card carrier. The full amount of your credit line is available to buy or lease goods or services where the card is honored. Part of your credit line, called the cash advance line, is available for cash advances. We may change your credit line or cash advance limit at any time for any reason. We will notify you of any change, but the change may take effect before you receive the notice. The total balance on your account, including periodic finance charges and fees, must always remain below the credit line. However, if the total balance exceeds your credit line you must still pay us. If your account has a credit balance, we may reduce the credit balance by any new charges on your account. You may not maintain a credit balance in excess of your credit line.

**Billing Statement:** Your billing statement shows the total balance, periodic finance charges, fees, minimum amount due, and payment due date. It also shows your current credit line and cash advance limit; an itemized list of current charges, payments and credits; a rate summary; and other important information. We deliver a statement to only one address. You must notify Customer Service of a change in address. If we deem your account uncollectible or institute collection proceedings by sending it to an outside agency or attorney for collection, we may stop sending you statements. Periodic finance charges and fees continue to accrue even if we stop sending statements.

The total amount you owe us appears as the New Balance on the billing statement. To determine the New Balance we begin with the total balance at the start of the billing period. We add any purchases or cash advances and subtract any credits or payments credited as of that billing period. We then add any periodic finance charges or fees and make other adjustments.

## APRs

**APRs Based on Prime:** We calculate any APR based on the U.S. Prime Rate ("Prime Rate") by adding the applicable amount that appears on the card carrier to the Prime Rate. For each billing period we use the Prime Rate published in The Wall Street Journal two business days prior to the Statement/Closing Date for that billing period. If The Wall Street Journal does not publish the Prime Rate, we may substitute a similar published rate. A change in an APR due to a change in the Prime Rate takes effect as of the first day of the billing period for which we calculate the APR. We apply the new applicable APR to any existing balances, subject to any promotional rate that may apply.

**Default Rate:** All your APRs may increase if you default under any Card Agreement that you have with us because you fail to make a payment to us when due, you exceed your credit line, or you make a payment to us that is not honored. In these circumstances, we may automatically increase your APRs (including any promotional APRs) on all balances to the Default APR, which equals the Prime Rate plus up to 23.99%, or up to 28.99%, whichever is greater. Factors considered in determining your Default APR may include how long your account has been open, the timing or seriousness of a default under any Card Agreement that you have with us, or other indications of account performance. The Default APR takes effect as of the first day of the billing period in which you default. We may lower the APR for new purchases and/or cash advances if you meet the terms of all Card Agreements that you have with us for six consecutive billing periods. Existing balances remain subject to the Default APR until paid in full, unless we tell you otherwise.

7

**Effect of APR Increases:** If an APR increases, periodic finance charges increase and your minimum payment may increase.

## Periodic Finance Charges Based On APRs

**Periodic Finance Charges:** Periodic finance charges are finance charges that are added to your account when we apply the applicable APR to the balances on your account. We calculate periodic finance charges separately for each balance subject to different terms, for example, standard purchases, standard cash advances, and each promotional offer. The total periodic finance charge for the billing period equals the daily periodic finance charges for each balance for each day in the billing period. This method of calculating periodic finance charges results in daily compounding of finance charges.

**When Periodic Finance Charges Begin to Accrue:** Periodic finance charges begin to accrue on a charge from the date it is added to the daily balance and continue to accrue until payment in full is credited to your account. (Charges include purchases, balance transfers, cash advances, transaction fees, other fees, and any minimum finance charge.) You can avoid periodic finance charges on purchases (excluding balance transfers) that appear on your current billing statement if you paid the New Balance on the last statement by the payment due date on that statement and you pay your New Balance by the payment due date on your current statement. If you made a balance transfer, you may be unable to avoid periodic finance charges on new purchases, as described in the balance transfer offer.

**Calculation of Periodic Finance Charges:**
- For each balance, we multiply the daily balance by the applicable daily periodic rate. We do this for each day in the billing period. A daily periodic rate is the applicable APR divided by 365. A billing period begins on the day after the Statement/Closing Date of the previous billing period and includes the Statement/Closing Date of the current billing period.

- To get the daily balance, we take the beginning balance for each balance every day (including unpaid periodic finance charges from previous billing periods), add any new charges, and any periodic finance charge on the previous day's balance, subtract any credits or payments credited as of that day, and make other adjustments. A credit balance is treated as a balance of zero.

- We add a charge to the daily balance as follows: We add a purchase to the appropriate balance as of the Sale Date on the billing statement. We add a balance transfer or cash advance to the appropriate balance as of the Post Date on the statement. We add any transaction fees for purchases,

balance transfers, or cash advances to the same balance as the transaction as of the same date the transaction is added to the daily balance. The Post Date is the date we receive your request for the balance transfer or cash advance, including a request that we complete a balance transfer or cash advance convenience check for a specific amount. If you send a balance transfer or convenience check directly to someone, the Post Date is the date we receive the check for payment.

- To get the total periodic finance charge, we add up all of the daily periodic finance charges for each balance for each day in the billing period.

- For each balance, the Balance Subject to Finance Charge on the statement is the average of the daily balances during the billing period. If you multiply this figure for each balance by the number of days in the billing period and by the applicable daily periodic rate, the result is the periodic finance charges assessed for that balance, except for minor variations caused by rounding.

**Minimum Finance Charge:** If the periodic rate finance charge would otherwise be less than $0.50, we assess a minimum FINANCE CHARGE of $0.50. We add this amount to any balance that is assessed a finance charge.

## Transaction Fees

**Transaction Fees and APRs:** If you are assessed a transaction fee for a balance transfer, a purchase made in a foreign currency, or a cash advance, the transaction fee will cause the APR on the billing statement on which the transaction first appears to exceed your nominal APR.

**Transaction Fee for Balance Transfers:** You obtain a balance transfer if you obtain funds through a balance transfer check or transfer a balance without using a cash advance convenience check. We treat balance transfers as purchases unless otherwise provided in this Agreement. For each balance transfer we add an additional FINANCE CHARGE of 3% of the amount of the balance transfer but not less than $5 or more than $75.

**Transaction Fee for Purchases Made in a Foreign Currency:** For each purchase made in a foreign currency we add an additional FINANCE CHARGE of 3% of the purchase amount after its conversion into U.S. dollars.

**Transaction Fee for Cash Advances:** You obtain a cash advance if you obtain funds through an automated teller machine (ATM), convenience check, home banking, or financial institution; make a wire transfer; obtain a money order, traveler's check, lottery ticket, casino chip, or similar item; or engage in a similar transaction. For each cash

29

advance we add an additional **FINANCE CHARGE** of 3% of the amount of the cash advance, but not less than $5.

## Other Fees

**Late Fee:** We add a late fee to the standard purchase balance for each billing period you fail to pay, by its due date, the Minimum Amount Due (less the Amount Over Credit Line shown on your billing statement). This fee is based on your account balance as of the payment due date. It is: $15 on balances up to $100, $29 on balances of $100 up to $250, and $39 on balances of $250 and over.

**Over-the-Credit-Line Fee:** We add a $39 fee to the standard purchase balance if your account balance exceeds your credit line at any time during the billing period. We add this fee even if transactions we authorize or periodic finance charges, fees, and other charges you incur are a reason the account balance exceeds your credit line. We add this fee even if the account balance falls below your credit line by the end of the billing period.

**Annual Membership Fee:** We add any applicable annual membership fee to the standard purchase balance. This fee is non-refundable unless you notify us to cancel your account within 30 days of the mailing or delivery date of the billing statement on which the fee is billed.

**Returned Payment Fee:** We add a $39 fee to the standard purchase balance if a payment check or similar instrument is not honored or is returned because it cannot be processed, or if an automatic debit is returned unpaid. We assess this fee the first time your check or payment is not honored, even if it is honored upon resubmission.

**Returned Convenience Check Fee:** We add a $39 fee to the standard advance balance if we decline to honor a convenience check. We may decline to honor these checks if, for example, the amount of the check would cause the balance to exceed the cash advance limit or credit line, if you default, if you did not comply with our instructions regarding the check, or if your account has been closed.

**Stop Payment on Convenience Check Fee:** We add a $39 fee to the standard advance balance if we honor your request to stop payment on a convenience check. To stop payment on a convenience check write us at P.O. Box 6000, Sioux Falls, South Dakota, 57117    call the Customer Service number on the billing statement. If you call, you must confirm the call in writing within 14 days. A written stop payment order remains in effect for 6 months unless renewed in writing.

**Balance Transfer Checks and Convenience Checks:** Each check must be in the form it was issued and used according

to any instructions we give. The checks must not be used to pay an amount owed us under this or another Card Agreement that you have with us. We do not certify these checks or return any such checks that have been paid.

## Information on Foreign Currency Conversion Procedures

If you make a transaction in a foreign currency, other than a cash advance made at a branch or ATM of one of our affiliates, MasterCard, Visa or American Express, depending on which card is used, converts the amount into U.S. dollars as follows:

- MasterCard complies with its foreign currency conversion procedures then in effect. MasterCard currently uses a conversion rate in effect one day prior to its transaction processing date. Such rate is either a wholesale market rate or the government-mandated rate.
- Visa complies with its foreign currency conversion procedures then in effect. Visa currently uses a conversion rate in effect on its applicable central processing date. Such rate is either a rate it selects from the range of rates available in wholesale currency markets, which may vary from the rate it receives, or the government-mandated rate.
- American Express complies with its foreign currency conversion procedures then in effect. Unless a particular rate is required by applicable law, the rate used by American Express shall be the highest interbank rate selected on the business day prior to the day on which the transaction is processed by American Express.

If a cash advance is made in a foreign currency at a branch or ATM of one of our affiliates, the amount is converted into U.S. dollars by our affiliate in accordance with its foreign currency conversion procedures then in effect. Our affiliate currently uses a conversion rate in effect on its applicable processing date. Such rate is either a mid-point market rate or the government-mandated rate.

The foreign currency conversion rate in effect on the applicable processing date for a transaction may differ from the rate in effect on the Sale or Post date on your billing statement for that transaction.

If a transaction is converted by a third party prior to such transaction being processed by MasterCard, Visa, or American Express, the foreign currency conversion rate for that transaction will be the rate selected by that third party.

## Payments

**Minimum Amount Due:** Each month you must pay at least the Minimum Amount Due by the payment due date. The sooner you pay the New Balance, the less you will pay in periodic finance charges.

To calculate the Minimum Amount Due, we begin with any past due amount and add any amount in excess of your credit line. We then add the largest of the following:

- The New Balance on the billing statement if it is less than $20;
- $20 if the New Balance is at least $20;
- 1% of the New Balance (which calculation is rounded down to the nearest dollar) plus the amount of your billed finance charges and any applicable late fee; or
- 1.5% of the New Balance (which calculation is rounded down to the nearest dollar).

However, the Minimum Amount Due never exceeds the New Balance. In calculating the Minimum Amount Due, we may subtract from the New Balance certain fees added to your account during the billing period.

**Application of Payments:** We apply payments and credits to low APR balances before higher APR balances. That means your savings will be reduced if you make transactions that are subject to higher APRs.

**Payment Instructions:** Payments are credited in accordance with the payment instructions on the billing statement. You must pay us in U.S. dollars using a check, similar instrument, or automatic debit that is drawn on and honored by a bank in the U.S. Do not send cash. We can accept late or partial payments, and payments that reflect "paid in full" or other restrictive endorsements, without losing our rights. We reserve the right to accept payments made in foreign currency and instruments drawn on funds on deposit outside the U.S. If we do, we select the currency conversion rate at our discretion and credit your account in U.S. dollars after deducting any costs incurred in processing your payment, or we may bill you separately for such costs.

**Optional Pay by Phone Service:** You may request to make your payment by phone using our optional Pay by Phone Service. Each time you make such a request, you agree to pay us the amount shown in the Pay by Phone section on the back of the billing statement. Our representatives are trained to tell you this amount if you decide to use this optional Pay by Phone Service.

### Credit Reporting

We may report information about your account to credit reporting agencies. Late payments, missed payments, or other defaults on your account may appear on your credit report. If you request cards on your account for others, we may report account information in the names of those other

people as well. We may also obtain follow-up credit reports on you (for example, when we review your account for a credit line increase). If you wish to know which agencies we contacted, write us at the Customer Service address on the billing statement.

If you think we reported erroneous information to a credit reporting agency, write us at the Customer Service address on the billing statement. We will promptly investigate the matter and if we agree with you, we will contact each credit reporting agency to which we reported and request a correction. If, after our investigation, we disagree with you, we will tell you in writing or by telephone and tell you how to submit a statement to those agencies for inclusion in your credit report.

### Changes to this Agreement

We may change the rates, fees, and terms of this Agreement at any time for any reason. These reasons may be based on information in your credit report, such as your failure to make payments to another creditor when due, amounts owed to other creditors, the number of credit accounts outstanding, or the number of credit inquiries. These reasons may also include competitive or market-related factors. Changing terms includes adding, replacing, or deleting provisions relating to your account and to the nature, extent, and enforcement of the rights and obligations you or we have relating to this Agreement. These changes are binding on you. However, if the change will cause a fee, rate or minimum payment to increase, we will mail you written notice at least 15 days before the beginning of the billing period in which the change becomes effective. If you do not agree to the change, you must notify us in writing within 25 days after the effective date of the change and pay us the total balance, either at once or under the terms of the unchanged Agreement. Unless we notify you otherwise, use of the card after the effective date of the change shall be deemed acceptance of the new terms, even if the 25 days have not expired.

### Default

You default under this Agreement if you fail to pay the Minimum Amount Due by its due date; exceed your credit line; pay by a check or similar instrument that is not honored or that we must return because it cannot be processed; pay by automatic debit that is returned unpaid; file for bankruptcy; or default under any other Card Agreement that you have with us. If you default, we may close your account and demand immediate payment of the total balance. If you gave us a security interest in a Certificate of Deposit, we may use the deposit amount to pay any amount you owe.

31

## Refusal of the Card, Closed Accounts, and Related Provisions

**Refusal of the Card:** We do not guarantee approval of transactions and are not liable for transactions that are not approved, either by us or by a third party, even if you have sufficient credit available. We may limit the number of transactions that may be approved in one day. If we detect unusual or suspicious activity, we may suspend your credit privileges until we can verify the activity.

**Preauthorized Charges:** If you default, if the card is lost or stolen, or we change your account for any reason, we may suspend automatic charges with third party vendors. If preauthorized charges are suspended, you are responsible for making direct payment for such charges until you contact the third party to reinstate the automatic charges.

**Lost or Stolen Cards, Account Numbers, or Convenience and Balance Transfer Checks:** If any card, account number, or check is lost or stolen or if you think someone used or may use them without permission, call us at the Customer Service number on the billing statement or the number obtained by calling toll-free or local Directory Assistance. We may require you to provide certain information in writing to help us find out what happened and to comply with our investigation. You must identify for us the charges that were not made by you, or someone authorized by you, and from which you received no benefit.

**Closing Your Account:** You may close your account by notifying us in writing or by calling toll-free at the Customer Service number shown on the billing statement or on the back of your credit card, but must still repay the total balance in accordance with this Agreement. We may close your account or suspend account privileges at any time for any reason without prior notice. We may also reissue a different card at any time. You must return any card to us upon request.

**Security Interest for Secured Accounts:** If your account is a secured account, you gave us a security interest in a Certificate of Deposit to secure repayment of your account. If you withdraw your funds from the Certificate of Deposit, we will close your account.

---

## ARBITRATION

*PLEASE READ THIS PROVISION OF THE AGREEMENT CAREFULLY.* IT PROVIDES THAT ANY DISPUTE MAY BE RESOLVED BY BINDING ARBITRATION. ARBITRATION REPLACES THE RIGHT TO GO TO COURT, INCLUDING THE RIGHT TO A JURY AND THE RIGHT TO PARTICIPATE IN A CLASS ACTION OR SIMILAR PROCEEDING. IN ARBITRATION,

A DISPUTE IS RESOLVED BY AN ARBITRATOR INSTEAD OF A JUDGE OR JURY. ARBITRATION PROCEDURES ARE SIMPLER AND MORE LIMITED THAN COURT PROCEDURES.

*Agreement to Arbitrate:* Either you or we may, without the other's consent, elect mandatory, binding arbitration for any claim, dispute, or controversy between you and us (called "Claims").

### Claims Covered

**What Claims are subject to arbitration?** All Claims relating to your account, a prior related account, or our relationship are subject to arbitration, including Claims regarding the application, enforceability, or interpretation of this Agreement and this arbitration provision. All Claims are subject to arbitration, no matter what legal theory they are based on or what remedy (damages, or injunctive or declaratory relief) they seek. This includes Claims based on contract, tort (including intentional tort), fraud, agency, your or our negligence, statutory or regulatory provisions, or any other sources of law; Claims made as counterclaims, cross-claims, third-party claims, interpleaders or otherwise; and Claims made independently or with other claims. A party who initiates a proceeding in court may elect arbitration with respect to any Claim advanced in that proceeding by any other party. Claims and remedies sought as part of a class action, private attorney general or other representative action are subject to arbitration on an individual (non-class, non-representative) basis, and the arbitrator may award relief only on an individual (non-class, non-representative) basis.

**Whose Claims are subject to arbitration?** Not only ours and yours, but also Claims made by or against anyone connected with us or you or claiming through us or you, such as a co-applicant or authorized user of your account, an employee, agent, representative, affiliated company, predecessor or successor, heir, assignee, or trustee in bankruptcy.

**What time frame applies to Claims subject to arbitration?** Claims arising in the past, present, or future, including Claims arising before the opening of your account, are subject to arbitration.

**Broadest Interpretation.** Any questions about whether Claims are subject to arbitration shall be resolved by interpreting this arbitration provision in the broadest way the law will allow it to be enforced. This arbitration provision is governed by the Federal Arbitration Act (the "FAA").

**What about Claims filed in Small Claims Court?** Claims filed in a small claims court are not subject to arbitration, so long as the matter remains in such court and advances only an individual (non-class, non-representative) Claim.

## How Arbitration Works

**How does a party initiate arbitration?** The party filing an arbitration must choose one of the following two arbitration firms and follow its rules and procedures for initiating and pursuing an arbitration: American Arbitration Association or National Arbitration Forum. Any arbitration hearing that you attend will be held at a place chosen by the arbitration firm in the same city as the U.S. District Court closest to your then current billing address, or at some other place to which you and we agree in writing. You may obtain copies of the current rules of each of the arbitration firms and forms and instructions for initiating an arbitration by contacting them as follows:

American Arbitration Association
335 Madison Avenue, Floor 10
New York, NY 10017-4605
Web site: www.adr.org

National Arbitration Forum
P.O. Box 50191
Minneapolis, MN 55405
Web site: www.arbitration-forum.com

At any time you or we may ask an appropriate court to compel arbitration of Claims, or to stay the litigation of Claims pending arbitration, even if such Claims are part of a lawsuit, unless a trial has begun or a final judgment has been entered. Even if a party fails to exercise these rights at any particular time, or in connection with any particular Claims, that party can still require arbitration at a later time or in connection with any other Claims.

**What procedures and law are applicable in arbitration?** A single, neutral arbitrator will resolve Claims. The arbitrator will be either a lawyer with at least ten years experience or a retired or former judge, selected in accordance with the rules of the arbitration firm. The arbitration will follow procedures and rules of the arbitration firm in effect on the date the arbitration is filed unless those procedures and rules are inconsistent with this Agreement, in which case this Agreement will prevail. Those procedures and rules may limit the discovery available to you or us. The arbitrator will take reasonable steps to protect customer account information and other confidential information if requested to do so by you or us. The arbitrator will apply applicable substantive law consistent with the FAA and applicable statutes of limitations, will honor claims of privilege recognized at law, and will have the power to award to a party any damages or other relief provided for under applicable law. You or we may choose to have a hearing and be represented by counsel. The arbitrator will make any award in writing and, if requested by you or us,

will provide a brief statement of the reasons for the award. An award in arbitration shall determine the rights and obligations between the named parties only, and only in respect of the Claims in arbitration, and shall not have any bearing on the rights and obligations of any other person, or on the resolution of any other dispute.

**Who pays?** Whoever files the arbitration pays the initial filing fee. If we file, we pay; if you file, you pay, unless you get a fee waiver under the applicable rules of the arbitration firm. If you have paid the initial filing fee and you prevail, we will reimburse you for that fee. If there is a hearing, we will pay any fees of the arbitrator and arbitration firm for the first day of that hearing. All other fees will be allocated as provided by the rules of the arbitration firm and applicable law. However, we will advance or reimburse your fees if the arbitration firm or arbitrator determines there is good reason for requiring us to do so, or if you ask us and we determine there is good reason for doing so. Each party will bear the expense of that party's attorneys, experts, and witnesses, and other expenses, regardless of which party prevails, but a party may recover any or all expenses from another party if the arbitrator, applying applicable law, so determines.

**Who can be a party?** Claims must be brought in the name of an individual person or entity and must proceed on an individual (non-class, non-representative) basis. The arbitrator will not award relief for or against anyone who is not a party. If you or we require arbitration of a Claim, neither you, we, nor any other person may pursue the Claim in arbitration as a class action, private attorney general action or other representative action, nor may such Claim be pursued on your or our behalf in any litigation in any court. Claims, including assigned Claims, of two or more persons may not be joined or consolidated in the same arbitration. However, applicants, co-applicants, authorized users on a single account and/or related accounts, or corporate affiliates are here considered as one person.

**When is an arbitration award final?** The arbitrator's award is final and binding on the parties unless a party appeals it in writing to the arbitration firm within fifteen days of notice of the award. The appeal must request a new arbitration before a panel of three neutral arbitrators designated by the same arbitration firm. The panel will consider all factual and legal issues anew, follow the same rules that apply to a proceeding using a single arbitrator, and make decisions based on the vote of the majority. Costs will be allocated in the same way they are allocated for arbitration before a single arbitrator. An award by a panel is final and binding on the parties after fifteen days has passed. A final and binding award is subject to judicial review and enforcement as provided by the FAA or other applicable law.

### Survival and Severability of Terms

This arbitration provision shall survive: (i) termination or changes in the Agreement, the account, or the relationship between you and us concerning the account; (ii) the bankruptcy of any party; and (iii) any transfer, sale or assignment of your account, or any amounts owed on your account, to any other person or entity. If any portion of this arbitration provision is deemed invalid or unenforceable, the entire arbitration provision shall not remain in force. No portion of this arbitration provision may be amended, severed or waived absent a written agreement between you and us.

### Applicable Law and Enforcing our Rights

**Applicable Law:** The terms and enforcement of this Agreement shall be governed by federal law and the law of South Dakota, where we are located.

**Enforcing this Agreement:** We can delay in enforcing or fail to enforce any of our rights under this Agreement without losing them.

**Collection Costs:** If we refer collection of your account to a lawyer who is not our salaried employee, you are liable for any reasonable attorney's fees we incur, plus the costs and expenses of any legal action, to the extent permitted by law.

**Assignment:** We may assign any or all of our rights and obligations under this Agreement to a third party.

### For Further Information

Call the toll-free Customer Service telephone number shown on the billing statement or on the back of your card. You can also call local or toll-free Directory Assistance to get our telephone number.

Ken Stork
President & CEO

Citibank (South Dakota), N.A.
P.O. Box 6000
Sioux Falls, SD 57117

© 2006 Citibank (South Dakota), N.A.

## What To Do If There's An Error In Your Bill.

*Your Billing Rights. Keep This Notice For Future Use.*
This notice contains important information about your rights and our responsibilities under the Fair Credit Billing Act.

*Notify Us In Case of Errors or Questions About Your Bill.*
If you think your billing statement is wrong, or if you need more information about a transaction on your billing statement, write to us (on a separate sheet) as soon as possible at the address provided in the Billing Rights Summary portion on the back of your statement. We must hear from you no later than 60 days after we sent you the first statement on which the error or problem appeared. You can telephone us, but doing so will not preserve your rights.

In your letter, give us the following information:
- Your name and account number.
- The dollar amount of the suspected error.
- Describe the error and explain, if you can, why you believe there is an error. If you need more information, describe the item you are unsure about.
- Please sign your letter.

If you authorized us to pay your credit card bill automatically from your savings or checking account, you can stop the payment on any amount you think is wrong. To stop the payment you must tell us at least three business days before the automatic payment is scheduled to occur.

*Your Rights and Our Responsibilities After We Receive Your Written Notice.*
We must acknowledge your letter within 30 days, unless we have corrected the error by then. Within 90 days, we must either correct the error or explain why we believe your billing statement was correct. After we receive your letter, we cannot try to collect any amount you question, or report your account as delinquent. We can continue to bill you for the amount you question, including finance charges, and we can apply any unpaid amount against your credit line. You do not have to pay any questioned amount while we are investigating, but you are still obligated to pay the parts of your balance that are not in question.

If we find that we made a mistake on your billing statement, you will not have to pay any finance charges related to any questioned amount. If we didn't make a mistake, you may have to pay finance charges, and you will have to make up any missed payments on the questioned amount. In either case, we will send you a statement of the amount you owe and the date it is due.

14

13

If you fail to pay the amount that we think you owe, we may report you as delinquent. However, if our explanation does not satisfy you and you write to us within 10 days telling us that you still refuse to pay, we must tell anyone we report you to that you have a question about your bill. And, we must tell you the name and address of anyone to whom we reported your account information. We must tell anyone we report you to that the matter has been settled between us when it is finally settled.

If we don't follow these rules, we can't collect the first $50 of the questioned amount, even if your billing statement was correct.

*Special Rule for Credit Card Purchases.*
If you have a problem with the quality of property or services that you purchased with a credit card, and you have tried in good faith to correct the problem with the merchant, you may have the right not to pay the remaining amount due on the property or services. There are two limitations on this right:

- You must have made the purchase in your home state or, if not within your home state, within 100 miles of your current address; and
- The purchase price must have been more than $50.

These limitations do not apply if we own or operate the merchant, or if we mailed you the advertisement for the property or services.

80491.70U   Pv. 57409  109000                                  05/05

16

# AFFIDAVIT

STATE OF MISSOURI

COUNTY OF PLATTE

Account Holder: SHEILA R. MUNOZ          Account No: XXXX-XXXX-XXXX-███

Social Security No: xxx-xx-███

The undersigned, *Crystal James* _____ being duly sworn, states and deposes as follows:

1. That s/he is an employee of Citicorp Credit Services, Inc. (USA) ("CCSI") located at 7920 NW 110th Street, Kansas City, MO 64153, and is authorized to make the statements and representations herein. CCSI is a subsidiary of Citibank (South Dakota), N.A. ("Citibank") and services credit card accounts for Citibank, including maintaining and recording information in Citibank's records as they relate to credit cards owned by Citibank. The statements set forth in this affidavit are true and correct to the best of my knowledge, information and belief based on either personal knowledge or review of the business records of Citibank and/or CCSI.

2. My duties include having knowledge of, and access to, business records relating to the Citibank account referenced above. These records are kept by CCSI on behalf of Citibank in the regular course of business and it was in the regular course of business of Citibank and/or CCSI for an employee or representative with personal knowledge of the act, event, condition, or opinion recorded to make memorandum or records or to transmit information thereof to be included in such memorandum or records; and that the records were made at or near the time of the act and/or event recorded or reasonably soon thereafter.

3. That CCSI, in the regular course of business, provides various credit card processing services to Citibank, including causing to be sent to customers periodic billing statements reflecting true and accurate activities on the customers' respective account(s) (other than months in which no statement may have been required by law).

4. That the records of Citibank indicate that account XXXX-XXXX-XXXX-███ was opened on, or acquired by Citibank on, 11/26/2004 in the name of SHEILA R. MUNOZ, with a Social Security Number with the last four digits ending in: xxx-xx-███ (Account).

5. That the records of Citibank indicate that as of the date the Account was sold, there was due and payable on the Account $13,171.06. The affiant further states that, to the best of his/her knowledge, information and belief there are no uncredited payments Owed to the Account.

6. That the records of Citibank indicate that the last payment on the account was made on 04/30/2007.

7: That the records of Citibank indicate that the record was sold to Asset Acceptance LLC on or about 06/29/2010 and Citibank retained no ownership interest in the account after it was sold.

**FURTHER AFFIANT SAYETH NOT.**

Dated this ___25___ day of __Ja___ 2011.

By: _____

Citicorp Credit Services, Inc. (USA)

Subscribed and sworn to before me this ___25___ day of __Ja___ , 2011 by _Krysta Davis_ an employee of Citicorp Credit Services, Inc. (USA)

_____
Notary Public

(Notary Stamp/Seal)

My Commission Expires: _____

## Chapter 2

# Finding the Weapons To Use in Defense

***Note:*** Asset Acceptance, LLC's, actual Summons and Complaint had attached to it three documents: Bill of Sale and Assignment, Card Member Agreement, and an Affidavit. These may be found at the end of this chapter, along with my Answer to their Complaint.

Let's take a look at the items attached to Asset Acceptance, LLC's, Summons and Complaint. Attached to the Complaint were three documents: a "Bill of Sale and Assignment," "Card Member Agreement," and an "Affidavit."

We will look at each one separately. Being good at fine details is a plus when looking over a Summons and a Complaint. The Complaint, especially any documentation attached to it, should be gone over with a fine-toothed comb. It should be compared to the Rules of Civil Procedure to see if they comply.

## 1. Bill of Sale and Assignment

In looking at Asset Acceptance, LLC's, "Bill of Sale and Assignment," I was able to glean some useful information that, in fact, came into important play later on in the lawsuit.

First of all, the title says "Bill of Sale and Assignment." It cannot be both. Either the debt is being retained by the original creditor and simply assigned to the JDB, or the debt was sold to the JDB and the original creditor no longer has a financial interest in the charged off debt.

So this brings a question that could be used in Discovery (next chapter): Was the alleged debt sold or assigned? This could possibly be an important point in a counterclaim, such as whether or not to sue the original creditor, along with Asset Acceptance, LLC, or simply sue Asset Acceptance, LLC.

If the debt was simply assigned, the original creditor has a financial interest in any collection of the charged off debt. The original creditor and the JDB will share in the proceeds of collected debt. If the JDB to whom the original creditor assigned the debt does not follow collection laws, the original creditor can be held responsible, also, in a counterclaim.

If the debt was sold to the JDB, was the debt purchased from another JDB or directly from the original creditor? The more the alleged debt is handed down from one JDB to another, the harder it is for the JDB to prove their case. Documents get lost or corrupted. Chain of custody of documentation would need to be proved by a live witness from each JDB each time the account was transferred from one JDB to the next and be available to testify and be cross examined.

If the debt has only been transferred to the first JDB from the original creditor, it would be up to the JDB to provide original documentation to prove their case, as well as produce a witness from the original creditor to validate the documentation. The witness would need to be present at the trial to be available for cross examination or the documentation may be deemed hearsay. Hearsay rules vary by state, but this information would be found in the Rules of Civil Procedure.

A Bill of Sale gives the date of when the debt was purchased. In Asset Acceptance, LLC's, Bill of Sale the date is June 29, 2010. This may be valuable information. In Florida, prior to October 1, 2010, the FCCPA stated that a JDB must give the consumer notice within 30 days that the debt has been purchased by them. Case law in Florida shows that cases have been dismissed with prejudice simply on a JDB not notifying the consumer within the 30-day time period. Florida courts have found that if a JDB acquired a debt prior to October 1, 2010, and failed to notify the consumer of the acquisition of the debt within 30 days, the debt is considered to be unbillable and uncollectable. In my case, it made all the difference in the world!

During Discovery I requested from Asset Acceptance, LLC, proof that they had notified me of their acquisition of the debt they were suing over. They sent me a copy of a letter from Asset Acceptance, LLC, on their letterhead, informing me of their acquisition of the debt. It was dated August 9, 2010, 41 days after they acquired the debt. The FCCPA stipulates it is to be done within 30 days.

> **Update:** On October 1, 2010, the Florida law was amended to read that a JDB must inform a consumer they have obtained the debt 30 days prior to any lawsuit being filed.

While looking at Asset Acceptance, LLC's, Bill of Sale, I asked myself, "Who signed the Bill of Sale? Are the signatures notarized? If not, how can one be sure the signatures are the signatures of whom they say they are?" This may possibly be a defense. These may be questions for Discovery. Learn to question everything!

In Asset Acceptance, LLC's, Bill of Sale, it states there is an Exhibit 1 attached which references the account that was sold or assigned. The Summons and Complaint did not have an Exhibit 1 attached. There is nothing in Asset Acceptance, LLC's, Bill of Sale that directly links this particular Bill of Sale to any specific account. How can one tell what account was sold or assigned by this Bill of Sale? This absolutely is a defense.

## 2. Card Member Agreement

Now, let's take a look at that Card Member Agreement Asset Acceptance, LLC, attached to their Complaint. First, one can see that it sets forth the possibility of Arbitration. If a Card Agreement allows for arbitration, the consumer would need to consider if Arbitration is a good option for them. As already stated, this book does not deal with Arbitration, but that does not mean it would not be a good choice for some. There are some excellent internet resources, especially forums, that give thorough information on this subject.

Most importantly, look at the date of the Card Member Agreement. In my case, Asset Acceptance, LLC, stated that the account was opened in 2004. However, the Card Member Agreement Asset Acceptance, LLC, was trying to use is 2006 (look at the last page and next to the last page of the Card Member Agreement). It was argued that credit card companies update their Card Member

Agreements from time to time. However, to use as a basis of a Complaint, a JDB should use the Card Member Agreement with the same date as when the alleged debt was begun. See what the judge said later in this book.

A third point concerning the Card Member Agreement Asset Acceptance, LLC, attached to their Complaint is that, again, there is no specific account linked with that specific Card Member Agreement. How can anyone tell that this or any other Card Member Agreement pertains to a specific account?

See how important looking for small details is when fighting against a JDB?

## 3. The Affidavit

This is where real headaches can start for the JDB! Ever hear of "robo-signing"? There is so much to point out in the Affidavit that was attached to Asset Acceptance, LLC's, Complaint.

The person signing the Affidavit, Crystal Janus, alleges she is an employee of the credit card company and that she signed the affidavit in Missouri. I researched "Crystal Janus" on the internet by name. There was only one Crystal Janus that came up over and over on the internet. The one and only Crystal Janus that came up from a Google search did not live in Missouri as stated in the Affidavit, but lived in Monroe, Michigan, less than one hour's drive from Asset Acceptance, LLC's, headquarters in Warren, Michigan. An employee?

In contrast, when I "Googled" my name, there were over 60 matches.

I never received an answer from Asset Acceptance, LLC, on this, as the case was voluntarily dismissed by Asset Acceptance, LLC, prior to their producing the legal identification and employer of Crystal Janus at the time the affidavit was signed as requested in Discovery.

Further research brought to the surface a deposition of an employee of Asset Acceptance, LLC, during which he revealed that employees of Asset Acceptance, LLC, including himself, in fact, did robo-sign affidavits on a regular basis, even signing them as quickly as one every 30 seconds.

Now, look at the signature page of the affidavit. Look at the notarization. I researched notarization rules. It varies state by state, but in Florida, as in most states, the notarization must include how the notary verified the identification of the person signing the affidavit. In this case, there is nothing that says the notary personally knew the signer or that identification (such as a driver's license) was provided as proof of identification. This notarization would most likely not hold up in Florida. How can one know "Crystal Janus" is not an alias? How can one know that this is not the 12-year-old child of an employee?

Remember, in a lawsuit, the Plaintiff (Asset Acceptance, LLC, in this case) is required to prove their case. The Defendant (consumer) only has to pierce the JDB's evidence. The consumer only has to raise a reasonable question to the JDB's accusations and/or their so-called evidence.

Asset Acceptance, LLC's, Affidavit referenced my account by the alleged credit card number. It was referenced by XXXX-XXXX-XXXX-####, where only the last four digits of the card number were given. Who, in their right mind, would be able to say with any certainty that, "Yes, this is definitely my account"? Only 25% of the account number is given. That leaves 75% room for error that this is my account to which this Affidavit is referring.

The full account number *was* given in Asset Acceptance, LLC's, Complaint; however, since so much time had passed, I no longer had any documentation to match against any account number(s) of mine to verify it. It was the responsibility of Asset Acceptance, LLC, to attach statements or other verification to the Complaint whereby I could identify as to whether or not the account belonged to me, per the Florida Rules of Civil Procedure.

With only four digits given in the Affidavit, how can I verify it matches the same account number given in the Complaint?

Asset Acceptance, LLC, gives an amount I supposedly owed them. There were no statements attached showing purchases, payments, interest, fees, etc.; there was no formulation given as to how the final amount supposedly owed was calculated. If I approached a neighbor and said, "Hey, friend, don't forget about the $25,000 you owe me," one would think he would question as to how I came up with the figure $25,000 and demand some type of proof that he owed me that.

These all bring up possible questions for Discovery.

## 4. "Exhibit 1" or "Exhibit A"

In Asset Acceptance, LLC's, Bill of Sale and Assignment in my case, it alluded to an Exhibit 1 that supposedly proved my specific account was sold to the JDB. However, in this case, there was no Exhibit 1 attached to Asset Acceptance, LLC's, Complaint. Later, at a hearing on the Motion To Strike Bill of Sale and Assignment, it was brought to the attention of the judge through the Motion To Strike Bill of Sale and Assignment that there was no Exhibit 1 attached to the Complaint. We will cover the hearing later.

In many lawsuits by JDBs, there is an "Exhibit 1" or "Exhibit A." It typically is a very simple spreadsheet that lists all of the debts in the portfolio that was purchased by the JDB at that one time. The spreadsheet is redacted to cover all the information except the information of the alleged debt in that specific lawsuit.

If there is such an Exhibit 1 or Exhibit A attached, it creates more questions than answers. A similar spreadsheet can be created by anyone with basic spreadsheet software knowledge. A list of names, account numbers, addresses, and amounts owed is hardly proof that a debt exists, to whom it belongs, or that the amount is in any way correct. Without the testimony of an employee of the original creditor and the availability of the witness for cross examination at the trial to verify the information, the spreadsheet would be considered hearsay in many courts. This is true for Florida. There would also need to be statements, receipts, cancelled checks, etc., to back up the amounts stated. However, in my case, although there was an Exhibit 1 alluded to, there was none attached to the Complaint.

Therefore, there was absolutely no proof whatsoever attached to Asset Acceptance, LLC's, lawsuit that backed up their claim against me. And to think I almost gave up at the very beginning and trashed the Summons and Complaint rather than answering it--just like approximately 90% of people do. Plus two attorneys had already advised me to pay the alleged debt ot file for bankruptcy (roll over and play dead)--they did not want to fight!

## BILL OF SALE AND ASSIGNMENT

THIS BILL OF SALE AND ASSIGNMENT is dated June 30, 2010, between Citibank (South Dakota), N.A., a national banking association organized under the laws of the United States, located at 701 East 60th Street North, Sioux Falls, SD 57117 (the "Bank") and Asset Acceptance, LLC ("Buyer"), organized under the laws of the Delaware, with its headquarters/principal place of business at 28405 Van Dyke Ave, Warren, MI 48093.

For value received and subject to the terms and conditions of the Purchase and Sale Agreement dated June 29, 2010, between Buyer and the Bank (the "Agreement"), the Bank does hereby transfer, sell, assign, convey, grant, bargain, set over and deliver to Buyer, and to Buyer's successors and assigns, the Accounts listed in Exhibit 1 and the final electronic file.

Citibank (South Dakota), N.A.

By: _____
(Signature)

Name: __Douglas C. Morrison__

Title: __Vice President & CFO__

Asset Acceptance, LLC

By: _____
(Signature)

Name: _____

Title: _____

The full Card Agreement may be found at the end of Chapter 1.
Here are only the last page and next to the last page
as referenced in Chapter 2.

to judicial review and enforcement as provided by the FAA or other applicable law.

**Survival and Severability of Terms**

This arbitration provision shall survive: (i) termination or changes in the Agreement, the account, or the relationship between you and us concerning the account; (ii) the bankruptcy of any party; and (iii) any transfer, sale or assignment of your account, or any amounts owed on your account, to any other person or entity. If any portion of this arbitration provision is deemed invalid or unenforceable, the entire arbitration provision shall not remain in force. No portion of this arbitration provision may be amended, severed or waived absent a written agreement between you and us.

**Applicable Law and Enforcing our Rights**

**Applicable Law:** The terms and enforcement of this Agreement shall be governed by federal law and the law of South Dakota, where we are located.

**Enforcing this Agreement:** We can delay in enforcing or fail to enforce any of our rights under this Agreement without losing them.

**Collection Costs:** If we refer collection of your account to a lawyer who is not our salaried employee, you are liable for any reasonable attorney's fees we incur, plus the costs and expenses of any legal action, to the extent permitted by law.

**Assignment:** We may assign any or all of your rights and obligations under this Agreement to a third party.

**For Further Information**

Call the toll-free Customer Service telephone number shown on the billing statement or on the back of your card. You can also call local or toll-free Directory Assistance to get our telephone number.

Ken Stork
President & CEO

Citibank (South Dakota), N.A.
P.O. Box 6000
Sioux Falls, SD 57117

**What To Do If There's An Error In Your Bill.**

*Your Billing Rights. Keep This Notice For Future Use.*
This notice contains important information about your rights and our responsibilities under the Fair Credit Billing Act.

*Notify Us In Case of Errors or Questions About Your Bill!*
If you think your billing statement is wrong, or if you need more information about a transaction on your billing statement, write to us (on a separate sheet) as soon as possible at the address provided in the Billing Rights Summary portion on the back of your statement. We must hear from you no later than 60 days after we sent you the first statement on which the error or problem appeared. You can telephone us, but doing so will not preserve your rights.

In your letter, give us the following information:
- Your name and account number.
- The dollar amount of the suspected error.
- Describe the error and explain, if you can, why you believe there is an error. If you need more information, describe the item you are unsure about.
- Please sign your letter.

If you authorized us to pay your credit card bill automatically from your savings or checking account, you can stop the payment on any amount you think is wrong. To stop the payment you must tell us at least three business days before the automatic payment is scheduled to occur.

*Your Rights and Our Responsibilities After We Receive Your Written Notice.*
We must acknowledge your letter within 30 days, unless we have corrected the error by then. Within 90 days, we must either correct the error or explain why we believe your billing statement was correct. After we receive your letter, we cannot try to collect any amount you question, or report your account as delinquent. We can continue to bill you for the amount you question, including finance charges, and we can apply any unpaid amount against your credit line. You do not have to pay any questioned amount while we are investigating, but you are still obligated to pay the parts of your balance that are not in question.

If we find that we made a mistake on your billing statement, you will not have to pay any finance charges related to any questioned amount. If we didn't make a mistake, you may have to pay finance charges, and you will have to make up any missed payments on the questioned amount. In either case, we will send you a statement of the amount you owe and the date it is due.

14

15

47

If you fail to pay the amount that we think you owe, we may report you as delinquent. However, if our explanation does not satisfy you and you write to us within 10 days telling us that you still refuse to pay, we must tell anyone we report you to that you have a question about your bill. And, we must tell you the name and address of anyone to whom we reported your account information. We must tell anyone we report you to that the matter has been settled between us when it is finally settled.

If we don't follow these rules, we can't collect the first $50 of the questioned amount, even if your billing statement was correct.

### Special Rule for Credit Card Purchases.

If you have a problem with the quality of property or services that you purchased with a credit card, and you have tried in good faith to correct the problem with the merchant, you may have the right not to pay the remaining amount due on the property or services. There are two limitations on this right:

- You must have made the purchase in your home state or, if not within your home state, within 100 miles of your current address; and
- The purchase price must have been more than $50.

These limitations do not apply if we own or operate the merchant, or if we mailed you the advertisement for the property or services.

48

# AFFIDAVIT

Account Holder: SHEILA R MUNOZ

Account No: XXXX-XXXX-XXXX ▮

Social Security No: xxx-xx- ▮

The undersigned, _Crystal James_ being duly sworn, states and deposes as follows:

1. That s/he is an employee of Citicorp Credit Services, Inc. (USA) ("CCSI") located at 7920 NW 110th Street, Kansas City, MO 64153, and is authorized to make the statements and representations herein. CCSI is a subsidiary of Citibank (South Dakota), N.A. ("Citibank") and services credit card accounts for Citibank, including maintaining and recording information in Citibank's records as they relate to credit cards owned by Citibank. The statements set forth in this affidavit are true and correct to the best of my knowledge, information and belief based on either personal knowledge or review of the business records of Citibank and/or CCSI.

2. My duties include having knowledge of, and access to, business records relating to the Citibank account referenced above. These records are kept by CCSI on behalf of Citibank in the regular course of business and it was in the regular course of business of Citibank and/or CCSI for an employee or representative with personal knowledge of the act, event, condition, or opinion recorded to make memorandum or records or to transmit information thereof to be included in such memorandum or records; and that the records were made at or near the time of the act and/or event recorded or reasonably soon thereafter.

3. That CCSI, in the regular course of business, provides various credit card processing services to Citibank, including causing to be sent to customers periodic billing statements reflecting true and accurate activities on the customers' respective account(s) (other than months in which no statement may have been required by law).

4. That the records of Citibank indicate that account XXXX-XXXX-XXXX ▮ was opened on, or acquired by Citibank on, 11/26/2004 in the name of SHEILA R MUNOZ, with a Social Security Number with the last four digits ending in: xxx-xx- ▮ (Account).

5. That the records of Citibank indicate that as of the date the Account was sold, there was due and payable on the Account $13,171.06. The affiant further states that, to the best of his/her knowledge, information and belief there are no uncredited payments Owed to the Account.

6. That the records of Citibank indicate that the last payment on the account was made on 04/30/2007.

7. That the records of Citibank indicate that the record was sold to Asset Acceptance LLC on or about 06/29/2010 and Citibank retained no ownership interest in the account after it was sold.

**FURTHER AFFIANT SAYETH NOT.**

Dated this _25_ day of _Ja___, 2011.

By: _____

Citicorp Credit Services, Inc. (USA)

Subscribed and sworn to before me this _25_ day of _Ja___, 2011 by _Krystel Jones_ an employee of Citicorp Credit Services, Inc. (USA)

_____
Notary Public

(Notary Stamp/Seal)

My Commission Expires: _____

# IN THE COUNTY COURT IN AND FOR POLK COUNTY, FLORIDA
## CIVIL DIVISION

ASSET ACCEPTANCE, LLC

      Plaintiff

vs.                          Case No. 5311CC1415

SHEILA R. MUNOZ,

      Defendant

## ANSWER TO COMPLAINT AND SUMMONS
## & AFFIRMATIVE DEFENSES

## ANSWER TO COMPLAINT AND SUMMONS

COMES NOW, the Defendant SHEILA R. MUNOZ, answers the Plaintiff, ASSET ACCEPTANCE, LLC, and answers:

1.      No knowledge of any damages.

2.      Agree.

3.      Agree.

4.      Disagrees.

5.      Disagrees.

6.      Disagrees.

7.      Defendant repeats and restates each and every material answer as contained in answers 1 through 6 above.

8.      Disagrees.

9.      Disagrees.

10.     Disagrees.

11.     Disagrees.

12.     Disagrees.

13.     Disagrees.

14.     Disagrees.

15.     Disagrees.

16.     Disagrees.

17.     Disagrees.

18.     Disagrees.

19.     Defendant repeats and restates each and every material answer as contained in answers 1 through 18 above.

20.     Disagrees.

21.     Disagrees.

22.     Disagrees.

## AFFIRMATIVE DEFENSES

FURTHER, the Defendant asserts the following defenses and states:

23.     The Plaintiff provided no validation of the alleged debt to the Defendant. There is no validation of a partial payment on or about April 30, 2007, including no validation of the amounts claimed to be owed by the Defendant. There were no copies of a signed Credit Card Agreement (contract), canceled checks, signed receipts, copies of any paper that show the Defendant agreed to pay what is allegedly owed.

24. Since the signatures on the Bill of Sale and Assignment have not been notarized, Defendant is not able to agree that the actual sale of the credit card account to the Plaintiff has occurred.

25. Plaintiff did not provide validation that an original Agreement was ever mailed to the Defendant.

26. Plaintiff did not provide validation that the Defendant ever signed a credit card and/or that the credit card was ever in the possession and/or control of the Defendant.

27. Plaintiff did not provide any validation of what the alleged amounts owed were for or how the amounts were calculated by providing canceled checks, signed receipts, copies of accounting procedures, etc.

28. Plaintiff did not provide any validation of receipt of periodic statements by the Defendant.

29. Plaintiff incurred no damages from the Defendant. Any alleged damages to the Plaintiff were self inflicted by knowingly purchasing an alleged debt that was already in default.

30. Plaintiff did not provide any validation of any business transactions between the Plaintiff and the Defendant.

31. WHEREFORE, the Defendant SHEILA R. MUNOZ respectfully requests the Court to dismiss the entire Complaint by Plaintiff ASSET ACCEPTANCE, LLC, with prejudice.

Dated _____ APRIL 19, _____, 2011

_____
SHEILA R. MUNOZ, Defendant

# CERTIFICATE OF SERVICE

I hereby certify that a copy hereof has been furnished by First Class Mail to Plaintiff's employee/attorney this _____ *19 TH* _____ day of April 2011, to the following address:

> Amanda R. Duffy
> Asset Acceptance, LLC
> PO Box 9065
> Brandon, FL 33509
> Fax No.: 813.983.2519

SHEILA R. MUÑOZ, Defendant

# Chapter 3

# Discovery

***Note:*** The actual Discovery documents from Asset Acceptance, LLC, to myself and my answers to their Discovery, as well as the actual Discovery documents from me to Asset Acceptance, LLC, and their answers may be found at the end of this chapter.

Discovery can be two-sided. The JDB will, most likely, send the consumer a Set of Interrogatories, a Request for Admissions, and a Request To Produce Documents. These collectively are called "Discovery." Of course, the Defendant (consumer) is allowed to send the JDB his own Set of Interrogatories, Request for Admissions, and a Request to Produce Documents. As it was in my case, it may possibly yield a gold mine of issues that can be used against the JDB and in the defense of the consumer. Keep in mind, JDBs are not used to having a consumer fight back and many times are not prepared to answer Discovery served on them by the consumer.

The purpose of Discovery is "you show me your case and I'll show you mine." Again, one must be sure to check the Rules of Civil Procedure for their state on Discovery. Some states may require motioning the court before sending Discovery. Florida does not. There may also be other restrictions, such as how many questions are allowed to be asked. One must be sure they are obeying the Rules for their respective state.

If possible, it may be strategically wise for a consumer to jump start and mail off Discovery to the JDB FIRST! There is a time limit (Rules of Civil Procedure) when Discovery must be answered by the other party. In Florida, I had 30 days plus an additional five days to answer Asset Acceptance, LLC's, Discovery, because it was mailed to me. The consumer may be able to get Discovery answers from the JDB (find out what "hand" the JDB is holding) before the consumer reveals to the JDB what the consumer is holding. One can always send additional Discovery requests later within the limits outlined by the Rules of Civil Procedure.

Discovery (the three documents mentioned above) itself is not filed with the court. One must file only the "Certificate of Service" with the court, letting the court know that Discovery has been served on the JDB. If the JDB does not respond timely, the court can be made aware of it. Again, it is wise to send Discovery to the JDB CMRRR so the JDB cannot say they did not receive it. One copy is retained by the consumer for their personal records; one Certificate of Service only is filed with the court; one set of Discovery with Certificate of Service is mailed to the attorney of the JDB.

The Answers to Discovery may not be required to be filed with the court. However, it is wise to go ahead and file them with the court anyway as proof that Discovery was timely answered. A Defendant should mail their answers to Discovery to the JDB's attorney CMRRR. A "Certificate of Service" is also attached. One copy is for the consumer's personal records; one copy is filed with the court; one copy is mailed to the JDB's attorney.

The same day I received Discovery from Asset Acceptance, LLC, I sent my own set of Discovery to them. These documents may all be found at the end of this chapter.

**Very important:** If Admissions are not answered within the proper timeframe, the answers are deemed "Admitted." I needed to watch the calendar!

Thirty-five long days passed while I waited for the answers to my Discovery requests to Asset Acceptance, LLC, to arrive. In Florida the time limit is 30 days with an additional five days if the mail is used for delivery. Of course, during that time I crafted my own answers to Asset Acceptance, LLC's, Discovery and got them sent off timely.

Thirty-six days and no answer from Asset Acceptance, LLC! Thirty-seven days, thirty-eight days . . . you get the idea.

Again, I looked to the Rules of Civil Procedure for a remedy. The Rules indicated that a party must make an attempt to contact the other side to "remind" them that Discovery was due before the party could initiate the court's help (Motion To Compel) to get their answers. A reminder letter was drawn up by myself (copy at end of chapter) and mailed to Asset Acceptance, LLC's, in-house attorney, Amanda Duffy, cc: the judge, as well as I left a voice message on Amanda Duffy's phone to the same effect. I gave Asset Acceptance, LLC, ten additional days to receive their answers to Discovery. On the tenth day after the date of the letter and phone call, I received Asset Acceptance, LLC's, answers to Discovery. Unbelievable!

Read the Discovery and answers of both sides of my case from the actual court documents found at the end of this chapter. From them, one may formulate their own Discovery as it pertains to their particular case.

Let's take a look at some of the issues that arose from Asset Acceptance, LLC's, answers to the Discovery served on them by myself:

## 1. First Set of Interrogatories to Asset Acceptance, LLC

Look at the last page. This is a sworn statement, notarized by the person answering the Interrogatories, Michele Cristiano-Cummins, a legal supervisor of Asset Acceptance, LLC. If one is not truthful in their answers, it would be perjury on their part.

In the first question, Asset Acceptance, LLC, states they are an assignee of the credit card company. However, in the Affidavit that was attached to the Complaint, it states the account was sold to Asset Acceptance, LLC, and that the original creditor retained no ownership interest in the debt. Now, which is it? This is "piercing the veil" of their evidence, poking holes.

In question 3, it may be important to know exactly who is answering the questions and what position they hold. In a counterclaim, one may want to add this person in the lawsuit, if appropriate. In many instances, individual employees and in-house attorneys may be sued as collectors, as well as the JDB company itself.

In question 4, it is important to know whom the JDB may call as a witness and to what matters they will be testifying. This is a good place to understand one's state's rules on hearsay. In Florida, the affidavit or other business records, such as bills or statements, are considered hearsay unless a witness who has personal knowledge of the affidavit or records is present to testify and be available for cross examination.

In my case, the person who signed the Affidavit that was attached to the Complaint, Crystal Janus, was not listed as a witness Asset Acceptance, LLC, intended to have present as a witness. That would deem the Affidavit as "hearsay" and inadmissible as evidence in court.

In question 7, if a counterclaim is filed, those working on attempted collection of an account may need to be added to the counterclaim as additional Defendants. Remember, in my case, since Asset Acceptance, LLC, had not notified me of their acquisition of the debt within 30 days, the debt is unbillable and uncollectable. Any attempt to collect on the debt (letters, phone calls, lawsuits) would be illegal. This author wonders if people being interviewed to work at debt collection facilities are told they can individually be sued by consumers.

Were all the questions in the Interrogatories fully answered? If not, a consumer may want to file a Motion To Compel, petitioning the court to compel the JDB to answer any questions not answered or not fully answered to the consumer's satisfaction in relation to the information the consumer is trying to obtain from the JDB.

I did not receive answers to all the questions or full answers to some questions from Asset Acceptance, LLC. I chose not to file a Motion To Compel as I believed it would extend the time of seeing an end to the lawsuit. Furthermore, I believed I already had enough issues to present to the court to win my case.

> *A Side Note:* The results of Question 7 proved interesting in my case: As will be discussed further in the next chapter, I ended up with no counterclaim in this case. However, after this case was voluntarily dismissed by Asset Acceptance, LLC, I filed a lawsuit against Asset Acceptance, LLC. In it, I originally named each of the five account representatives as defendants, as well as others. What happened with these five names is quite interesting.

When I filed a lawsuit against Asset Acceptance, LLC, the Process Server attempted to serve a separate Summons and Complaint on each of the defendants at Asset Acceptance, LLC's, Brandon/Riverview office. The Process Server was told that one of the account representatives, Scott Anderson was actually an alias for Scott Burkes. The Process Server was further told that two of the account representatives, Jessica Felix and Jenna Wood, were supposedly unknown to anyone working there. Did Michele Cristiano-Cummins give false information in the Interrogatories, or did the attorney and other employees of Asset Acceptance, LLC, give the Process Server false information when she attempted to serve the Summons and Complaints?

That means in answering the interrogatories as she did, Michele Cristiano-Cummins, as the legal supervisor for Asset Acceptance, LLC, either perjured herself or the two "unknowns" were also aliases to which they did not want to admit. Either way, the answers to the interrogatories contained false information, given under oath by Michele Cristiano-Cummins and notarized.

How would the court look at this if brought before a judge?

## 2. Request to Asset Acceptance, LLC, for Admissions

I carefully chose questions for Admissions that, if answered truthfully by Asset Acceptance, LLC, would narrow down the issues at hand in the lawsuit. When the lawsuit is first filed, there are a certain number of issues on which the Plaintiff is complaining or suing and a number of issues for which the Defendant is defending against or, in the case of a counterclaim, suing. By executing Discovery and/or motions, many or all of these issues may be absolved before trial. If the case ends up going all the way to a trial, the issues that are tried by the judge and/or jury are those issues that are left standing in which the Plaintiff and Defendant have not been able to come to an agreement or those the judge did not already rule on through Motions.

Hopefully, some admissions may come to light that may help the consumer to defend oneself, offer basis on which to sue (counterclaim), or get the case dismissed altogether.

Notice Asset Acceptance, LLC's, answer to question 1. The Florida Rules of Civil Procedure require the contract (written agreement) to be attached to the "Breach of Contract" Complaint. There was no contract attached. Asset Acceptance, LLC, did not attach a contract but, rather, refers to the Card Agreement. Remember, the Card Agreement was the wrong one. Neither did the Card Agreement refer to any specific alleged account. The Card Agreement cannot replace a contract.

In question 3, Asset Acceptance, LLC, admits I had no signed agreement (contract or account) with them. I never agreed to pay Asset Acceptance, LLC, anything on an account. If I never agreed to pay Asset Acceptance, LLC, on any account, how can there be a "Breach of Contract"? Remember, it is about poking holes in the JDB's case.

Not all states have a notification law. But Florida does. Prior to October 1, 2010, when a JDB acquired a debt from the original creditor or from another JDB, the FCCPA stipulated that the JDB must give the consumer notice within 30 days that they are the new owners of the debt. Without this 30-day notice, the case may be dismissed with prejudice as the debt is considered unbillable and uncollectable. Therefore, question 4 is addressing this issue.

After October 1, 2010, there is still a notification law on Florida law books. It changed to read that a JDB must give notice to the consumer that they purchased or was assigned the debt at least 30 days prior to filing a lawsuit in order to attempt to collect on the debt.

Here, Asset Acceptance, LLC, denies notice was not given, but now I could request proof of the notice in my Request To Produce Documents in order to check if the notification was within the 30 days. We will see later that in my case, the notice was given 41 days after Asset Acceptance, LLC, purchased the debt. This is grounds on which a Motion To Dismiss or a Motion for Summary Judgment with Prejudice may be granted.

In answer to question 5, Asset Acceptance, LLC, denies they have no documentation to prove I owed the debt. However, Asset

Acceptance, LLC, did not attach any of that documentation to the Complaint as required by Florida Rules of Civil Procedure. Later, they even issued a Subpoena to the original creditor for the documentation.

Questions 7 and 8 are geared toward proving Asset Acceptance, LLC's, alleged "damages" are not what they claim in their Complaint. Remember, a JDB purchases junk debt for typically 3% or less. If the alleged debt was never paid, the JDB would only be "damaged" by the amount of money they lost in the deal. But in the scope of the entire portfolio of junk debt they purchased wherein 90% of the consumers never even answer a Summons and Complaint, the JDB's profit is huge; there are no damages sustained.

In my case, the alleged debt was most likely purchased for approximately $300 or less. Yet, Asset Acceptance, LLC, claimed damages of approximately $14,000 with an additional $11,000 in interest and fees. Their actual "damages" are not more than what they paid for the debt. Any possible damages were brought on by themselves by purchasing what they already knew to be a "junk debt." That would amount to something like a person buying a known defective product, then suing the manufacturer for the defective product. This is an affirmative defense in regard to the amount Asset Acceptance, LLC, is alleging I owed them.

Question 13 brings up the fact that this approximate $300 paid to the original creditor for the alleged debt should have gone against the debt. It was payment on the debt. Was it subtracted from the amount allegedly owed by me?

Question 17 was attempting to get Asset Acceptance, LLC, to admit that they did not attach the proper documentation (i.e., the original contract) to the Complaint. Here Asset Acceptance, LLC, denies the allegation; however, the contract or statements, notes, etc., were not attached to the Complaint as required by the Florida Rules of Civil Procedure. This becomes an affirmative defense.

## 3. Request to Asset Acceptance, LLC,To Produce Documents

Over and over in Asset Acceptance, LLC's, response to my request to produce certain documents, Asset Acceptance, LLC, stated they do not have the documentation in their possession. What? How can they sue a consumer with no proof? More affirmative defenses.

All of the new defenses that came to light during Discovery were grounds to file a Motion To Dismiss or a Motion for Summary Judgment with Prejudice. The Motions would simply state the ground(s) on which the motion is being requested, with an attached Memorandum that goes into detail, quoting law and/or naming court cases to back up the stand. Again, this may vary somewhat by state. Check the Rules of Civil Procedure.

## 4. Asset Acceptance, LLC's, First Set of Interrogatories to Me

Basically, I provided only my name and address, which Asset Acceptance, LLC, already had. I did not reveal personal information, such as Social Security number, date of birth, place of employment, etc., as this information is needed only if and when a judgment would be ordered against me by the court. To answer these questions to Asset Acceptance, LLC, would be an invasion of my privacy. I had no idea where this information may end up, possibly causing my identity to be stolen.

I also did not want to help prove the case for Asset Acceptance, LLC. Remember, it is the JDB's full responsibility to prove their case. It is the consumer's job to poke holes in any evidence they supposedly have.

## 5. Asset Acceptance, LLC's, Request to Me for Admissions

In many states, including Florida, the Rules of Civil Procedure prohibit a consumer to simply say in essence that they do not know when asked by a JDB to admit something. The answer must reflect that the consumer at least checked into a possible answer.

I admitted in what county I resided (Asset Acceptance, LLC, already knew this), but on the remainder of the requested admissions, I simply stated that "after a reasonable inquiry, the information known or readily obtainable by me is insufficient to enable me to admit or deny this request."

## 6. Asset Acceptance, LLC's, Request to Me To Produce Documents

Again, it is the JDB's responsibility to prove their case. I was not required to nor wanted to help Asset Acceptance, LLC, prove their case. Therefore, I objected to each and every request to provide documentation. Asset Acceptance, LLC, already should have had the documentation in their possession, as it is on what they based their Complaint in the first place.

The following pages contain my Discovery
(Interrogatories, Request for Admissions, and
Request To Produce Documents)
to Asset Acceptance, LLC.

IN THE COUNTY COURT IN AND FOR POLK COUNTY, FLORIDA
CIVIL DIVISION

ASSET ACCEPTANCE, LLC

      Plaintiff

vs.                                 Case No. 5311CC1415

SHEILA R. MUNOZ,

      Defendant

## NOTICE OF SERVICE OF
## DEFENDANT'S INTERROGATORIES TO PLAINTIFF

Pursuant to Fl.R.Civ.P.1.340, Defendant, Sheila R. Munoz, PRO SE, hereby propounds Interrogatories to the Plaintiff, Asset Acceptance, LLC, number 1 through 18, to be answered in writing, under oath, or objected to within thirty (30) days of the date herein.

## CERTIFICATE OF SERVICE

I HEREBY CERTIFY that a true and correct copy of this face sheet has been filed with the clerk of court and an original and one copy of the foregoing, inclusive of the attached interrogatories, have been mailed to Plaintiff's attorney this 9th day of May, 2011, to the following address:

Amanda R. Duffy
Asset Acceptance, LLC
PO Box 9065
Brandon, FL 33509

SHEILA R. MUNOZ, Defendant

# FIRST SET OF INTERROGATORIES TO PLAINTIFF

1.      Is Asset Acceptance, LLC, the direct assignee of Citibank, or is Asset Acceptance, LLC, an assignee of an assignee? If there are additional assignees, identify each assignee, their business address, and telephone number.

2.      Identify when the alleged account was originally opened by the Defendant and when the alleged debt was charged off by Citibank.

3.      Identify the person or persons answering these interrogatories. Include their business address, business phone number, and title within the Plaintiff's organization.

4.     Provide the following information for each person known to the Plaintiff who has knowledge of facts relevant to this case, including, but not limited to, all persons interviewed by you or by any person cooperating with you in this action, giving a brief description thereof, for each person you may call as a witness in this case.

a.     Name, address, and telephone number
b.     Place of employment
c.     Relation to the Plaintiff
d.     The subjects and substance of the testimony the witness will give and whether the witness is to be tendered as an expert witness.

5.     Provide the following information:

a.     Your full name
b.     Your full business name
c.     Your business purpose (e.g., Creditor, Lender, Collection Agency, etc.)

6.      In regards to the contract or agreement alleged in this action, please state the following:

a.      Terms of the contract or agreement
b.      Credit limit amount in the alleged contract or agreement
c.      Date and monetary value of any valuable consideration received on the contract or agreement
d.      Date and monetary value of any payments or credits alleged to be executed on the contract or agreement.

7.      Provide the following information for each person who has had any involvement in any manner in any efforts on your behalf to collect or attempt to collect any debt(s) purportedly owing by Defendant.

a.      His/her position
b.      His/her work address, telephone number(s)
c.      Nature and purpose of his/her involvement

8.      Identify the persons or entities regarding any debt which you have attempted to collect from the Defendant. Identify all documents related or relevant to your contractual agreement(s) (servicing, assignments, etc.), or other business relationships with said persons or entities.

9.     Identify each person who has had any contact or communication on your behalf regarding Defendant's purported debt. State when, how, where, and with whom said contact or communication occurred and in detail and with particularity the substance thereof.

10.     Describe all collection activities which you were authorized to perform for Asset Acceptance, LLC, and identify the terms of the agreement between Asset Acceptance, LLC, and you pursuant to which you sought to collect this account.

11.     Describe Asset Acceptance, LLC's, procedure and policy with respect to the maintenance, preservation, chain of custody, and destruction of documents, stating in your answer whether any documents or things relating to any information requested in these interrogatories or related in any way to this lawsuit have ever been destroyed or are no longer in your custody. For each such document, please identify the document, how, when, and why each document was destroyed or otherwise left your control, the identity of any person who participated in any way in the destruction, and/ or action for destroying the document or to transfer it out of your control or custody; and if the document still exists, identify the person now having control or custody of the document.

12.     What document states in writing in support of your complaint that the Defendant is indebted to pay Asset Acceptance, LLC, and when was this agreed statement in writing entered into?

13.     On what date did the Defendant allegedly become indebted to Asset Acceptance, LLC, for $13,171.06 plus interest of $10,253.94?

14.     Identify all witnesses with evidence in support of your complaint that the Defendant entered into a contract and is indebted to Asset Acceptance, LLC.

15.     State all actions taken to verify the accuracy and completeness of the accounts reported and state your procedures designed to assure the maximum possible accuracy of the information reported by you.

16.     What is the date that the Defendant allegedly defaulted on the original account?

17.     What was the status of the alleged account when acquired?

18.    What credit card purchases and/or cash advances were made on this account, and when was each transaction made?


_____
                                                Plaintiff


STATE OF FLORIDA

COUNTY OF _____

        BEFORE ME, the undersigned authority, personally appeared _____, who being by me first duly sworn, deposes and says that he/she executed the foregoing Answers to Interrogatories and that they are true and correct to the best of his/her knowledge and belief.



_____
NOTARY PUBLIC,
STATE OF FLORIDA
ID PRODUCED   [    ]
TYPE OF ID PRODUCED:



_____
PRINT NAME

IN THE COUNTY COURT IN AND FOR POLK COUNTY, FLORIDA
CIVIL DIVISION

ASSET ACCEPTANCE, LLC

     Plaintiff

vs.                          Case No. 5311CC1415

SHEILA R. MUNOZ,

     Defendant

## NOTICE OF SERVICE OF
## DEFENDANT'S REQUEST FOR ADMISSIONS

YOU ARE NOTIFIED that the undersigned has served Request for Admissions on Plaintiff, Asset Acceptance, LLC, on this 9th day of May, 2011.

## CERTIFICATE OF SERVICE

I HEREBY CERTIFY that a true and correct copy of the foregoing was mailed to Plaintiff's attorney this 9th day of May, 2011, to the following address:

Amanda R. Duffy
Asset Acceptance, LLC
PO Box 9065
Brandon, FL 33509

_____
SHEILA R. MUNOZ, Defendant

# DEFENDANT'S REQUEST FOR ADMISSIONS TO PLAINTIFF

Defendant, Sheila R. Munoz, PRO SE, pursuant to Fl.R.Civ.P. 1.370, demands that Plaintiff, Asset Acceptance, LLC, admits or denies the truth of the following statements within thirty (30) days of this request.

1.    That there is no written agreement, signed by the Defendant, between Defendant and Citibank.

2.    That there is no written agreement, signed by the Defendant, between Plaintiff and Defendant.

3.    That pursuant to Fair Debt Collection Practices Act, 559.715, a credit card holder is authorized to pay the original creditor until receipt of notification of assignment of rights to payment and that payment is to be made to the assignee.

4.    That Defendant was not given any notification of assignment of the account or assignment of rights in regard to the alleged debt.

5.    That as of the date Plaintiff drafted their complaint, they had no evidence admissible at trial that proves Defendant owes the debt.

6.    That Asset Acceptance, LLC, is considered a Debt Collector under the Fair Debt Collection Practices Act.

7.    That if Asset Acceptance, LLC, did purchase the alleged account, it was known by the Plaintiff to be in default at the time of purchase.

8.    If this assignment is proven by Plaintiff, that it was purchased for less than the amount submitted in Plaintiff's complaint.

9.    That Plaintiff was not assigned Citibank's obligations under a purchase agreement.

10.    That Plaintiff is barred under the Fair Debt Collection Practices Act, 1692 f(1), from collecting interest on any amount not authorized by the agreement creating the debt or permitted by law.

11.    That Plaintiff does not have documents to claim the amount(s) allegedly owed as submitted in the complaint.

12.    That Plaintiff does not have a copy of or the original Citibank Cardholder Agreement (the one provided with the Complaint is dated 06/06, and it is alleged the agreement was made 11/04).

13.    That Citibank received payment from the Plaintiff for a purported debt, or a portion of the purported debt, or received other compensation in the form of monies or credits from the Plaintiff.

14.    That Crystal Janus is an employee of Asset Acceptance, LLC.

15.    That Asset Acceptance, LLC, did not transfer the alleged assignment rights over to Amanda R. Duffy for the purpose of collecting on the alleged debt.

16.    That Amanda R. Duffy is the real party in interest.

17.    That Plaintiff's attorney failed to comply with Fl.R.Civ.P. 1.130.

18.    That this debt is time-barred.

IN THE COUNTY COURT IN AND FOR POLK COUNTY, FLORIDA
CIVIL DIVISION

ASSET ACCEPTANCE, LLC

     Plaintiff

vs.                        Case No. 5311CC1415

SHEILA R. MUNOZ,

     Defendant

## NOTICE OF SERVICE OF DEFENDANT'S REQUEST FOR PRODUCTION OF DOCUMENTS TO PLAINTIFF

YOU ARE NOTIFIED that the undersigned has served Request for Production of Documents on Plaintiff, Asset Acceptance, LLC, on this 9th day of May, 2011, by First Class Mail.

## CERTIFICATE OF SERVICE

I HEREBY CERTIFY that a true and correct copy of the foregoing was furnished by First Class Mail to Plaintiff's attorney this 9th day of May, 2011, to the following address:

Amanda R. Duffy
Asset Acceptance, LLC
PO Box 9065
Brandon, FL 33509

_____
SHEILA R. MUNOZ, Defendant

# REQUEST FOR PRODUCTION OF DOCUMENTS
## TO PLAINTIFF

Defendant, Sheila R. Munoz, PRO SE, pursuant to Fl.R.Civ.P. 1.350, demands that Plaintiff, Asset Acceptance, LLC, produce at Defendant's address, ███████████████████████ the following documents within thirty (30) days of service of this request.

## ITEMS TO BE PRODUCED

1.      The actual credit card contract upon which your complaint is based.

2.      The contract, agreement, assignment, or other means of demonstrating that the Plaintiff has the authority and is legally entitled to collect on the alleged debt.

3.      The original or copy of the Purchase and Sale Agreement dated June 29, 2010, showing under what terms and conditions the alleged sale was done.

4.      Proof that Asset Acceptance, LLC, is registered in the State of Florida as a debt collection agency and proof of their required surety bond for the State of Florida.

5.      Evidence authorization of Plaintiff and attorney to do business, create loans, issue or extend credit, collect debts, and/or operate as a financial business in the State of Florida.

6.      Evidence proof of the Defendant's alleged debt to Plaintiff, including specifically the alleged contract between Citibank and the Defendant bearing Defendant's signature and that legally requires the Defendant to pay the actual amount entered into the complaint.

7.      The original or copy of the account agreement that states interest rate, grace period, finance charge, assignment, and specifically the State Laws under which the agreement and account are governed, plus other important facts.

8.     The Record of Assignment that shows the amount paid and/ or consideration due for the alleged account.

9.     An itemized account of all transactions and dates, showing credit card purchases and/or cash advances made on this alleged account.

10.    All copies of manuals, procedures, and protocols used by Plaintiff regarding communication with Citibank regarding purchased debt.

11.    Document(s) that prove Citibank sent the Defendant a notification of assignment of the account or assignment of rights.

12.    Any and all notices sent to Defendant by Citibank in regards to this account demanding payment.

13.    All copies of all statements generated while this alleged account was open with Citibank.

14.    A complete and accurate history of the interest charged on this alleged account with Citibank. Show the exact dates interest rates changed and list the various rates that were charged during this alleged debt and the method of amortization.

15.    Any and all notices sent to Defendant by Citibank announcing changes in interest, fees, or penalties, and/or the terms of this alleged debt.

16.    Identify each Credit Reporting Agency (credit bureau) to which the Plaintiff reported Defendant's alleged debt and the dates of each such report.

17.    The original dunning letter that was sent to Defendant.

18.    Any and all notices sent to Defendant by Citibank in regards to the alleged account announcing transfer and/or assignment of credit card account from Citibank to any collection agency or collection attorney.

19.    A copy of the agreement with Citibank that grants Amanda R. Duffy the authority to collect this alleged debt.

June 14, 2011

Amanda R. Duffy
Asset Acceptance, LLC
PO Box 9065
Brandon, FL 33509
Fax: 813.983.2519

      RE:    Asset Acceptance, LLC vs. Sheila R. Munoz, Case #5311CC1415

Dear Ms. Duffy:

This letter is in compliance with the requirement that I attempt to informally resolve a discovery dispute prior to bringing a Motion To Compel Discovery.

On May 9, 2011, you were served with Defendant's Interrogatories to Plaintiff, Defendant's Request for Admissions to Plaintiff, and Defendant's Request for Production of Documents, which were due no later than June 13, 2011. To date, you have utterly failed to respond.

Please advise me by June 24, 2011, as to your position regarding the requested discovery. Failing a response, I will file a Motion To Compel. For your convenience, I have provided a copy of all three requests with this letter.

I hereby certify that this letter, along with copies of the first three requests were faxed to the above fax number June 14, 2011, as well as the hard copy of this letter mailed by First Class mail to the Plaintiff's attorney at the above address.

Sincerely,

███████████████

Sheila R Munoz

███████████████

The following pages contain Asset Acceptance, LLC's, responses to my Discovery.

*Note:* Asset Acceptance, LLC, did not respond to my Discovery in a timely manner, as will be described later in the book. Their response was due no later than June 13, 2011 (30 days plus an additional five days for mailing). They were not mailed to me until June 23, 2011.

In addition, Asset Acceptance, LLC's, responsesto Questions 12-18 of the Interrogatories were never received by me.

For organizational purposes, however, I am putting Asset Acceptance, LLC's, responses to my Discovery as I received them here, rather than chronologically when they were actually received.

# IN THE COUNTY COURT IN AND FOR POLK COUNTY, FLORIDA
## CIVIL DIVISION

ASSET ACCEPTANCE LLC,

      Plaintiff,

vs.                        Case No: 53 2011-CC-1415

SHEILA R. MUNOZ,

      Defendant.
_____/

## PLAINTIFF'S NOTICE OF SERVICE OF
## ANSWERS TO DEFENDANT'S FIRST SET OF INTERROGATORIES

**YOU ARE NOTIFIED** that the undersigned has served Answers to Defendant's

First Set of Interrogatories upon Defendant on this __23__ day of ~~May~~ June, 2011.

## CERTIFICATE OF SERVICE

**I HEREBY CERTIFY** that a true and correct copy of the foregoing was furnished by regular U.S. mail to Sheila R. Munoz, *Defendant,* ▉▉▉▉▉▉▉▉▉▉▉▉▉▉▉▉▉▉▉▉▉▉▉▉▉, on this __23__ day of ~~May~~ June, 2011.

                         _____
                         { }Rodolfo J. Miro, Bar-0103799
                         { }Anthony J. Steele, Bar-0074810
                         {X}Amanda Duffy, Bar - 0035612
                         Staff Attorneys for Plaintiff
                         P.O. Box 9065
                         Brandon, FL 33509
                         (813) 569-0518

AALLC REF. NO.: 10-400001837

# IN THE COUNTY COURT IN AND FOR POLK COUNTY, FLORIDA
## CIVIL DIVISION

ASSET ACCEPTANCE LLC,

      Plaintiff,

vs.                         Case No: 53 2011-CC-1415

SHEILA R. MUNOZ,

      Defendant.

## PLAINTIFF'S ANSWERS TO
## DEFENDANT'S FIRST SET OF INTERROGATORIES

1. Is Asset Acceptance, LLC, the direct assignee of Citibank or is Asset Acceptance, LLC, an assignee of an assignee? If there are additional assignees, identify each assignee, their business address, and telephone number.

   **Direct assignee from Citibank (South Dakota), N.A.**

2. Identify when the alleged account was originally opened by the Defendant and when the alleged debt was charged off by Citibank.

   **Citibank account number ▉▉▉▉▉▉▉▉▉▉ was opened November 26, 2004 and charged off December 4, 2007.**

3. Identify the person or persons answering these interrogatories. Include their business address, business phone number, and title within the Plaintiff's organization.

   **Michelle Cristiano-Cummins-Legal Supervisor.**
   **2840 S. Faulkenburg Rd., Riverview, FL 33578**
   **(813) 569-0810**

4. To Provide the following information for each person known to the Plaintiff who has knowledge of facts relevant to this case, including, but not limited to, all persons interviewed by you or by any person cooperating with you in this action, giving a brief description thereof, for each person you may call as a witness in this case.

   a. Name, address, and telephone number: **Michelle Cristiano-Cummins, 2840 S. Faulkenburg Rd., Riverview, FL 33578 (813) 569-0810**
   b. Place of employment : **Asset Acceptance, LLC**

5. Provide the following information:
   a. Your full name **Michelle Cristiano-Cummins**
   b. Your full business name **Asset Acceptance, LLC**
   c. Your business purpose (e.g., Creditor, Lender, Collection Agency, etc.)
      **Creditor and Consumer Collection Agency**

6. In regards to the contract or agreement alleged in this action, please state the following:
   a. Terms of the contract or agreement.
   b. Credit limit amount in the alleged contract or agreement.
   c. Date and monetary value of any valuable consideration received on the contract or agreement.
   d. Date and monetary value of any payments or credits alleged to be executed on the contract or agreement.
      **See attached card member agreement.**

7. Provide the following information for each person who has had any involvement in any manner in any efforts on your behalf to collect or attempt to collect any debt(s) purportedly owing by Defendant.
   a. His/her position.
   b. His/her work address, telephone numbers.
   c. Nature and purpose of his/her involvement.
   **Jenna Wood, Account Representative, 2840 S. Faulkenburg Rd., Riverview, FL 33578; 866-266-7660; Attempted telephone contact with Defendant on 08/20/2010**
   **Scott Meyer, Account Representative, 2840 S. Faulkenburg Rd., Riverview, FL 33578; 866-266-7660; Attempted telephone contact with Defendant on 09/27/2010.**
   **Scott Anderson, Account Representative, 2840 S. Faulkenburg Rd., Riverview, FL 33578; 866-266-7660; Attempted telephone contact with Defendant on 10/06/2010.**
   **Jessica Felix, Account Representative, 2840 S. Faulkenburg Rd., Riverview, FL 33578; 866-266-7660; Attempted telephone contact with Defendant on 11/26/2010.**
   **Denise Owens, Account Representative, 2840 S. Faulkenburg Rd., Riverview, FL 33578; 866-266-7660; Attempted telephone contact with Defendant on 03/17/2011.**
   **Colleen Ashley, Legal Assistant, 2840 S. Faulkenburg Rd., Riverview, FL 33578; 813-569-0810; prepared and mailed legal documents.**
   **Amanda R. Duffy, Esq., Staff Attorney, 2840 S. Faulkenburg Rd., Riverview, FL 33578; 813-569-0810.**

8. Identify the persons or entities regarding any debt which you have attempted to collect from Defendant. Identify all documents related or relevant to your contractual agreement(s) (servicing, assignments, etc.), or other business relationships with said persons or entities.
**See No. 7 above and**
**See documents provided with Plaintiff's Response to Defendant's Request for Production of Documents**

9. Identify each person who has had any contact or communication on your behalf regarding Defendant's purported debt. State when, how, where, and with whom said contact or communication occurred and in detail and with particularity the substance thereof.
**See No. 7 above**

10. Describe all collection activities which you were authorized to perform for Asset Acceptance, LLC, and identify the terms of the agreement between Asset Acceptance, LLC, and you pursuant to which you sought to collect this account.
**I am an employee, legal supervisor, for Asset Acceptance, LLC.**

11. Describe Asset Acceptance, LLC's, procedure and policy with respect to the maintenance, preservation, chain of custody, and destruction of documents, stating in your answer whether any documents or things relating to any information requested in these interrogatories or related in any way to this lawsuit have ever been destroyed or are no longer in your custody. For each such document, please identify the document, how, when and why each document was destroyed or otherwise left your control, the identify of any person who participated in any way in the destruction, and/or action for destroying the document or to transfer it out of your control or custody; and if the document still exists, identify the person now having control or custody of the document.
**Documents are retained electronically.**

STATE OF FLORIDA )
COUNTY OF HILLSBOROUGH )

**BEFORE ME,** the undersigned authority, personally appeared Michelle Cristiano-Cummins, who being by me first duly sworn, deposes and says that she executed the foregoing Answers to Interrogatories and that they are true and correct to the best of her knowledge and belief.

_____
NOTARY PUBLIC, STATE OF FLORIDA
AT LARGE

Personally Known          [ ] Print name _____

## IN THE COUNTY COURT IN AND FOR POLK COUNTY, FLORIDA
## CIVIL DIVISION

ASSET ACCEPTANCE LLC,

        Plaintiff,

vs.

                      ·Case No: 53 2011-CC-1415

SHEILA R. MUNOZ

        Defendant.

_____/

### PLAINTIFF'S ANSWERS TO
### DEFENDANT'S FIRST REQUEST FOR ADMISSIONS

Plaintiff, ASSET ACCEPTANCE LLC, by and through its undersigned attorneys,

hereby submits its written answers to Defendant's First Request for Admissions as

follows:

1. That there is no written agreement, signed by the Defendant, between Defendant and Citibank.

   **Can neither admit or deny. Discovery is ongoing. In addition, the terms of the card member agreement, of which were ratified by Defendant's acceptance and use of the credit card, creates an implied contract based on the express writing in the card member agreement. Malsby v. Gamble, 61 Fla. 310, 61 Fla. 327, 54 So. 766 (Fla. 1911); Gateway Cable T.V., Inc. v. Vikoa Constr. Corp., 253 So. 2d 461 (Fla 1st D.C.A. 1972); Scocozzo v. General Dev. Corp., 191 So. 2d 572 (Fla. 4th D.C.A. 1966), Head v. Lane, 495 So. 2d 821. 824 (Fla. 4th D.C.A. 1986).**

2. That there is no written agreement, signed by the Defendant, between Plaintiff and Defendant.

   **Admit.**

3. That pursuant to Fair Debt Collection Practices Act, 559.715, a credit card holder is authorized to pay the original creditor until receipt of notification of assignment of rights to payment and that payment is to be made to the assignee.

   **Admit.**

4. That Defendant was not given any notification of assignment of the account or assignment of rights in regard to the alleged debt.
   **Deny.**

5. That as of the date Plaintiff drafted their complaint, they had no evidence admissible at trial that proves Defendant owes the debt.
   **Deny.**

6. That Asset Acceptance, LLC, is considered a Debt Collector under the Fair Debt Collection Practices Act.
   **Admit.**

7. That if Asset Acceptance, LLC did purchase the alleged account, it was known by the Plaintiff to be in default at the time of purchase.
   **Admit.**

8. If this assignment is proven by Plaintiff that it was purchased for less than the amount submitted in Plaintiff's complaint.
   **Object. Vague. Plaintiff does not understand what Defendant is alleging.**

9. That Plaintiff was not assigned Citibank's obligations under a purchase agreement.
   **Deny.**

10. That Plaintiff is barred under the Fair Debt Collection Practices Act, 1692 f(1), from collecting interest on any amount not authorized by the agreement creating the debt or permitted by law.
    **Admit.**

11. That Plaintiff does not have documents to claim the amount(s) allegedly owed as submitted in the complaint.
    **Deny.**

12. That Plaintiff does not have a copy of or the original Citibank Cardholder Agreement (the one provided with the Complaint is dated 06/06, and it is alleged the agreement was made 11/04).
    **Deny.**

13. That Citibank received payment from the Plaintiff for a purported debt, or a portion of the purported debt, or received other compensation in the form of monies or credits from the Plaintiff.
    **Object. Vague.**

14. That Amanda R. Duffy is an employee of Asset Acceptance, LLC.

**Admit.**

15. That Asset Acceptance, LLP did not transfer the alleged assignment rights over to Amanda R. Duffy for the purpose of collecting on the alleged debt.
    **Admit.**

16. That Amanda R. Duffy is the real party in interest.
    **Deny.**

17. That Plaintiff's attorney failed to comply with Florida R 1.130.
    **Deny.**

18. That this debt is time-barred.
    **Deny.**

## CERTIFICATE OF SERVICE

I HEREBY CERTIFY that a true and correct copy of the foregoing has been

furnished by regular U.S. mail to Sheila R. Munoz, *Defendant,* ▮▮▮▮▮▮▮▮▮

▮▮▮▮▮▮▮▮ , on this _23_ day of ~~May~~ June, 2011.

{ }Rodolfo J. Miro, Bar-0103799
{ }Anthony J. Steele, Bar-0074810
{X}Amanda Duffy, Bar-0035612
Staff Attorneys for Plaintiff
P.O. Box 9065
Brandon, FL 33509
(813) 569-0518

# IN THE COUNTY COURT IN AND FOR POLK COUNTY, FLORIDA
## CIVIL DIVISION

ASSET ACCEPTANCE LLC,

      Plaintiff,

vs.                          Case No: 53-2011-CC-001415

SHEILA R. MUNOZ,

      Defendant.

_____/

## PLAINTIFF'S NOTICE OF SERVICE OF
## RESPONSE TO DEFENDANT'S REQUEST TO PRODUCE

**YOU ARE NOTIFIED** that the undersigned has served Responses to Defendant's Request to Produce upon Defendant, on this _23_ day of June, 2011.

## CERTIFICATE OF SERVICE

**I HEREBY CERTIFY** that a true and correct copy of the foregoing was furnished by regular U.S. mail to Sheila R. Munoz, *Defendant,* ████████████ ████████████████ , this _23_ day of June, 2011.

 

                ( ) Rodolfo J. Miro, Bar No. 0103799
                ( ) Anthony J. Steele, Bar No. 0074810
                ( ) Howard Butler, Bar No. 0753041
                (X) Amanda Duffy, Bar No. 0035612
                Staff Attorney for Plaintiff
                ASSET ACCEPTANCE LLC
                P.O. BOX 9065
                BRANDON, FL 33509
                (866) 266-7660
                (813) 983-2519 facsimile

# IN THE COUNTY COURT IN AND FOR POLK COUNTY, FLORIDA
## CIVIL DIVISION

ASSET ACCEPTANCE LLC,

      Plaintiff,

vs.                      Case No: 53-2011-CC-001415

SHEILA R. MUNOZ,

      Defendant.
_____/

## PLAINTIFF'S RESPONSES TO
## DEFENDANT'S REQUEST TO PRODUCE

Plaintiff, ASSET ACCEPTANCE LLC, responds to Defendant's Request to Produce as

follows:

1. The actual credit card contract upon which your complaint is based.

    **RESPONSE: Citibank (South Dakota), N.A. card agreement is attached. Discovery is ongoing. Plaintiff reserves the right to supplement its response to this Request at a later date.**

2. The contract, agreement, assignment, or other means of demonstrating that the Plaintiff has the authority and is legally entitled to collect on the alleged debt.

    **RESPONSE: Copy of Affidavit of Citicorp Credit Services, Inc., a subsidiary of Citibank (South Dakota), N.A. dated January 25, 2011; Copy of Bill of Sale from Citibank (South Dakota), N.A. to Asset Acceptance, LLC dated June 29, 2010; Schedule "A", and Citibank (South Dakota), N.A. card agreement are attached.**

3. The original or copy of the Purchase and Sale Agreement dated June 29, 2010 showing under what terms and conditions the alleged sale was done.

    **RESPONSE: Object. The Request seeks information that is protected by trade secret and/or proprietary in nature.**

4. Proof that Asset Acceptance, LLC, is registered in the State of Florida as a debt collection agency and proof of their required surety bond for the State of Florida.

    **RESPONSE: State of Florida Consumer Collection Agency License information and Hillsborough County Business License are attached.**

5. Evidence authorization of Plaintiff and attorney to do business, create loans, issue or extend credit, collect debts, and/or operate as a financial business in the State of Florida.

   **RESPONSE: State of Florida Consumer Collection Agency License information and Hillsborough County Business License are attached.**

6. Evidence proof of the Defendant's alleged debt to Plaintiff, including specifically the alleged contract between Citibank and the Defendant bearing Defendant's signature and that legally requires the Defendant to pay the actual amount entered into the complaint.

   **RESPONSE: Copy of Affidavit of Citicorp Credit Services, Inc., a subsidiary of Citibank (South Dakota), N.A. dated January 25, 2011; Copy of Bill of Sale from Citibank (South Dakota), N.A. to Asset Acceptance, LLC dated June 29, 2010; Schedule "A", and Citibank (South Dakota), N.A. card agreement are attached. Discovery is ongoing. Plaintiff reserves the right to supplement this response at a later date.**

7. The original or copy of the account agreement that states interest rate, grace period, finance charge, assignment, and specifically the State Laws under which the agreement and account are governed, plus other important facts.

   **RESPONSE: Citibank (South Dakota), N.A. card agreement is attached.**

8. The Record of Assignment that shows the amount paid and/or the consideration due for the alleged account.

   **RESPONSE: Copy of Affidavit of Citicorp Credit Services, Inc., a subsidiary of Citibank (South Dakota), N.A. dated January 25, 2011; Copy of Bill of Sale from Citibank (South Dakota), N.A. to Asset Acceptance, LLC dated June 29, 2010; Schedule "A", and Citibank (South Dakota), N.A. card agreement are attached. Object to the remainder of Request as irrelevant and not likely to lead to the discovery of admissible evidence.**

9. An itemized account of all transactions and dates, showing credit card purchases and/or cash advances made on this alleged account.

   **RESPONSE: Defendant is requesting payments, histories, and/or applications of funds transmitted between Defendant and Citibank, a non-party. Any payment(s), histories, applications of funds between Defendant and Citibank are not currently in Plaintiff's possession. Copy of Affidavit of Citicorp Credit Services, Inc., a subsidiary of Citibank (South Dakota), N.A. dated January 25, 2011; Copy of Bill of Sale from Citibank (South Dakota), N.A. to Asset Acceptance, LLC dated June 29, 2010 and Schedule "A" reflecting the charge-off amount and interest are attached. Discovery is ongoing. Plaintiff reserves the right to supplement its response to this Request at a later date.**

10. All copies of manuals, procedures, and protocols used by Plaintiff regarding communication with Citibank regarding purchased debt.

   **RESPONSE: Objection. The Request in overly broad and unduly burdensome and protected by work product privilege. Further, the Request seeks information that is irrelevant, confidential, trade secret, and proprietary in nature.**

11. Document(s) that prove Citibank sent the Defendant a notification of assignment of the account or assignment of rights.

   **RESPONSE: Defendant is requesting documentation transmitted from Citibank, a non-party, to Defendant. Any documentation from Citibank to Defendant is not in Plaintiff's possession. The First Notice Letter from Plaintiff to Defendant dated August 9, 2010 is attached.**

12. Any and all notices sent to Defendant by Citibank in regards to this account demanding payment.

   **RESPONSE: Objection. Defendant is requesting documentation transmitted from Citibank, a non-party, to Defendant. Any documentation from Citibank to Defendant is not in Plaintiff's possession. The First Notice Letter from Plaintiff to Defendant dated August 9, 2010 is attached. Notification of lawsuit letter from Plaintiff to Defendant dated 4/11/2011 is attached. Discovery is ongoing. Plaintiff reserves the right to supplement its response to this Request at a later date.**

13. All copies of all statements generated while this alleged account was open with Citibank.

   **RESPONSE: Discovery is ongoing. Statements will be produced when received by Plaintiff.**

14. A complete and accurate history of the interest charged on this alleged account with Citibank. Show the exact dates interest rates changed and list the various rates that were charged during this alleged debt and the method of amortization.

   **RESPONSE: Discovery is ongoing. Statements will be produced when received by Plaintiff.**

15. Any and all notices sent to Defendant by Citibank announcing changes in interest, fees, or penalties, and/or the terms of this alleged debt.

   **RESPONSE: Objection. Defendant is requesting documentation transmitted from Citibank, a non-party, to Defendant. Any documentation from Citibank to Defendant is not in Plaintiff's possession. The First Notice Letter from Plaintiff to Defendant dated August 9, 2010 is attached.**

16. Identify each Credit Reporting Agency (credit bureau) to which the Plaintiff reported Defendant's alleged debt and the dates of each such report.

   **RESPONSE: We do not report alleged debts to the credit bureaus. We furnish data about our accounts to the Credit Reporting Agencies Equifax, Experian**

and TransUnion. Data about the subject account was furnished to the Credit Reporting Agencies on 9/9/10, 10/30/10, 12/30/10, 2/5/11, 36/6/11, 4/17/11, 4/24/11, 5/8/11, and 6/12/11.

17. The original dunning letter that was sent to Defendant.

   **RESPONSE: Objection. The Request is vague. The First Notice Letter from Plaintiff to Defendant dated August 9, 2010 is attached.**

18. Any and all notices sent to Defendant by Citibank in regards to account, announcing transfer and/or assignment of credit card account from Citibank to any collection agency or collection attorney.

   **RESPONSE: Objection. Defendant is requesting documentation transmitted from Citibank, a non-party, to Defendant. Any documentation from Citibank to Defendant is not in Plaintiff's possession. The First Notice Letter from Plaintiff to Defendant dated August 9, 2010 is attached.**

19. A copy of the agreement with Citibank that grants Amanda R. Duffy the authority to collect his alleged debt.

   **RESPONSE: Objection. Amanda R. Duffy is the attorney of record for Plaintiff. Plaintiff has the right to collect the debt in virtue of the assignment. Copy of Affidavit of Citicorp Credit Services, Inc., a subsidiary of Citibank (South Dakota), N.A. dated January 25, 2011; Copy of Bill of Sale from Citibank (South Dakota), N.A. to Asset Acceptance, LLC dated June 29, 2010; Schedule "A", and Citibank (South Dakota), N.A. card agreement are attached.**

## CERTIFICATE OF SERVICE

   **I HEREBY CERTIFY** that a true and correct copy of the foregoing was furnished by regular U.S. mail to Sheila R. Munoz, *Defendant,* ███████████████████, on this 23 day of June, 2011.

   ( ) Rodolfo J. Miro, Bar No. 0103799
   ( ) Anthony J. Steele, Bar No. 0074810
   ( ) Howard Butler, Bar No. 0753041
   (X) Amanda Duffy, Bar No. 0035612
   Staff Attorney for Plaintiff
   ASSET ACCEPTANCE LLC
   PO BOX 9065
   BRANDON FL 33509
   (866) 266-7660
   (813) 983-2519 facsimile

10-400001837

# Asset Acceptance, LLC

August 9, 2010                                                                                         First Notice

Re: CITIBANK
Original Acct #: ████████████
Asset Acceptance, LLC Acct #: 10-400001837
Balance Past Due: $21640.95

Dear Sheila R Munoz:

It is our pleasure to welcome you as a new customer of Asset Acceptance, LLC. Your account with the above mentioned creditor has been purchased and is now owned by Asset Acceptance, LLC. In order to insure proper credit for any payments it is necessary that all future payments and inquiries be made to: Asset Acceptance, LLC, PO BOX 2036, Warren, MI 48090-2036.

Unless you notify this office within 30 days after receiving this notice that you dispute the validity of this debt or any portion thereof, this office will assume this debt is valid. If you notify this office in writing within 30 days from receiving this notice, this office will: obtain verification of the debt or obtain a copy of a judgment and mail you a copy of such judgment or verification. If you request this office in writing within 30 days after receiving this notice this office will provide you with the name and address of the original creditor, if different from the current creditor.

**This is an attempt to collect a debt and any information obtained will be used for that purpose.**

Sincerely,

Christi Wright Phone: 877-692-6188 Ext. 0
Debt Collector
Asset Acceptance, LLC

We may report information about your account to credit bureaus. Correspondence concerning inaccuracies and disputes relating to your credit report should be sent to: P.O. Box 1630 Warren, MI 48090-1630.

See Reverse Side for Important Information Regarding Privacy Policy

---

***Detach Lower Portion and Return with Payment***                                  ICGASSE01_OS_0328

PO Box 2039
Warren MI 48090-2039
ADDRESS SERVICE REQUESTED

Asset Acceptance, LLC Acct #: 10-400001837
Balance Past Due: $21640.95

August 9, 2010

10-400001837-OS_0328          172514
‖'‖'‖‖ı'ıı'‖‖ıₙ'‖‖'ıₙ'‖'‖ıₙₙₙₙ'ı'ıₙ‖'‖'ₙ'ₙ'ı‖'‖'ₙ'‖'
Sheila R Munoz
████████████████

Asset Acceptance, LLC
PO Box 2036
Warren MI 48090-2036
ıₗ'ı'ₙ‖'ₗₗ'‖'ₙₙ'ₗₗ'ₗ'ₙₙₙₗ'‖'ₗ'ₙₙ'‖'ₗₗ'ₙₙ'‖'ₗ'ₗₗ'ₗ'ₗ'ₗ'

95

The following pages contain
Asset Acceptance, LLC's, Discovery
(Interrogatories, Request for Admissions, and
Request To Produce Documents)
to me, along with my Answers to their Discovery.

***Note:*** Asset Acceptance, LLC's, Discovery, and my Answers
to their Discovery are herein combined
in order to conserve space and avoid redundancy.

IN THE COUNTY COURT IN AND FOR POLK COUNTY, FLORIDA
CIVIL DIVISION

ASSET ACCEPTANCE, LLC

     Plaintiff

vs.                       Case No. 5311CC1415

SHEILA R. MUNOZ,

     Defendant

## NOTICE OF SERVICE OF
## ANSWER TO FIRST SET OF INTERROGATORIES

YOU ARE NOTIFIED that the undersigned has served Answers to First Set of Interrogatories to Plaintiff, Asset Acceptance, LLC, on this 9th day of June, 2011, by First Class Mail.

## CERTIFICATE OF SERVICE

I HEREBY CERTIFY that a true and correct copy of the foregoing was mailed to Plaintiff's attorney this 9th day of June, 2011, to the following address:

Amanda R. Duffy
Asset Acceptance, LLC
PO Box 9065
Brandon, FL 33509

_____

SHEILA R. MUNOZ, Defendant

# FIRST SET OF INTERROGATORIES TO DEFENDANT

1.      Please state your full name, social security number, date
of birth, current home address, home telephone number, place of
employment, address of place of employment, and position held at
place of employment.

*Sheila R. Munoz*

███████████████████████████

*Supplication of additional information here is objected to by the
Defendant on grounds that it seeks information that is invasive of
the Defendant's privacy [Fl.R.Civ.P. 1.280(b)(1)] and is irrelevant
to any issue in this action, information  not calculated to lead
to the discovery of evidence, and would result in the disclosure
of information where such disclosure would violate the privacy
rights of the Defendant.*

2.      Please state each and every address you have resided at since
November 26, 2004, as well as the beginning and ending dates that
you resided at each address.

*Objected to by the Defendant on grounds that it seeks information
that is invasive of the Defendant's privacy [Fl.R.Civ.P. 1.280(b)
(1)] and is irrelevant to any issue in this action, information  not
calculated to lead to the discovery of evidence.*

3.      Set forth the full name, street address, and telephone
number of each and every individual who has knowledge, or claims
to have knowledge concerning the allegations contained in the
Plaintiff's Complaint or any defense or counter claims thereto, and
set forth the information held by each individual.

*Objected to by Defendant to the extent that it is seeking
information that is premature, given that the parties are in the
midst of discovery and pertinent documents have not yet been
produced by the Plaintiff. The Defendant cannot possibly answer
this interrogatory when she has not seen the Plaintiff's answers to
her discovery.*

*Without waiving her objection, the Defendant, upon completion of discovery with the Plaintiff, will most definitely have defenses in this action and will provide such defenses to the Plaintiff if asked through discovery. The Defendant reserves the right to update this answer to this interrogatory at a later time when that decision is made.*

4,     Set forth the full name, street address, and telephone number of each and every individual you intend to call to testify at trial in this cause.

*Objected to by Defendant to the extent that it is seeking information that is premature, given that the parties are in the midst of discovery and pertinent documents have not yet been produced by the Plaintiff. The Defendant cannot possibly answer this interrogatory when she has not seen the Plaintiff's answers to her discovery.*

*Without waiving her objection, the Defendant at this time has no witnesses, but reserves the right to call witnesses, if need be, once the Plaintiff answers the discovery given by the Defendant.*

5.     Identify by name and location, each and every document that you intend to offer or proffer into evidence in this cause.

*Objected to by Defendant to the extent that it is seeking information that is premature, given that the parties are in the midst of discovery and pertinent documents have not yet been produced by the Plaintiff.*

*Without waiving her objection, the Defendant at this time has no documents to offer into evidence, but reserves the right to offer documents, if need be, once the Plaintiff answers the discovery given by the Defendant.*

6.     Please state whether Defendant purchased goods and services on the Citibank credit card account that is the subject matter of the Plaintiff's Complaint.

*Objected to by Defendant on the grounds that Plaintiff's request should be accessible to Plaintiff from Plaintiff's own files, from documents or information already in Plaintiff's possession.*

7.     Please state whether Defendant made any payments on the account that is the subject matter of Plaintiff's Complaint. If yes, state the number of payments and the amount of each payment. Attach any evidence of payments that supports your statements made herein.

*Objected to by Defendant on the grounds that it is overly broad, unduly burdensome, cumulative, and/or duplicative to the extent it seeks documents or records that are not within the current knowledge, possession, custody, or control of the Defendant. Plaintiff's request should be accessible to Plaintiff from Plaintiff's own files, from documents or information already in Plaintiff's possession. The Plaintiff did not attach a copy of the alleged contract and/or pertinent documents evidencing alleged charges to the Complaint [Fl.R.Civ.P. 1.130(a)], thus the probity of the requested information is speculative. The Defendant has sought the alleged contract, along with other alleged pertinent documents, on the account that is the subject matter of Plaintiff's Complaint through discovery and demands strict proof thereof.*

*Without waiving the Defendant's objection, the Defendant, to the best of her knowledge, has never made any payments on the alleged account that is the subject of the Plaintiff's Complaint.*

8.     Please state the name and address of each banking institution at which you have held any accounts from November 26, 2004, to December 4, 2007, the types of accounts held at each institution, the beginning and ending dates you held the account, and the corresponding accounts' numbers.

*Objected to by the Defendant on grounds that it seeks information that is invasive of the Defendant's privacy [Fl.R.Civ.P. 1.280(b) (1)] and is irrelevant to any issue in this action, information not calculated to lead to the discovery of evidence, and would result in the disclosure of information where such disclosure would violate the privacy rights of the Defendant.*

9.      Please state whether the Defendant received statements, bills, invoices, or dunning notices requesting payment on the account that is the subject matter of the Plaintiff's Complaint.

*Objected to by Defendant on the grounds that it is overly broad, unduly burdensome, cumulative, and/or duplicative to the extent it seeks documents or records that are not within the current knowledge, possession, custody, or control of the Defendant. Plaintiff's request should be accessible to Plaintiff from Plaintiff's own files, from documents or information already in Plaintiff's possession. The Plaintiff did not attach a copy of the alleged contract and/or pertinent documents evidencing alleged charges to the Complaint [Fl.R.Civ.P. 1.130(a)], thus the probity of the requested information is speculative. The Defendant has sought the alleged contract, along with other alleged pertinent documents, on the account that is the subject matter of Plaintiff's Complaint through discovery and demands strict proof thereof.*

*Without waiving the Defendant's objection, the Defendant, to the best of her knowledge, has never received statements, bills, invoices, or dunning notices on the alleged account that is the subject matter of the Plaintiff's Complaint.*

10.      Please state whether the Defendant disputed the charges submitted by Citibank for purchases made on the account that is the subject matter of Plaintiff's Complaint. If in writing, please attach all documentation.

*Objected to by Defendant on the grounds that it is overly broad, unduly burdensome, cumulative, and/or duplicative to the extent it seeks documents or records that are not within the current knowledge, possession, custody, or control of the Defendant. Plaintiff's request should be accessible to Plaintiff from Plaintiff's own files, from documents or information already in Plaintiff's possession. The Plaintiff did not attach a copy of the alleged contract and/or pertinent documents evidencing alleged charges to the Complaint [Fl.R.Civ.P. 1.130(a)], thus the probity of the requested information is speculative. The Defendant has sought the alleged contract, along with other alleged pertinent documents, on the account that is the subject matter of Plaintiff's Complaint through discovery and demands strict proof thereof.*

a.) If yes, please state the name of Defendant and/or representation of the Defendant who communicated the dispute, the representative of Citibank and/or Asset Acceptance, LLC, to whom the dispute was communicated, and the dates on which the dispute was communicated.

*Objected to by Defendant on the grounds that it is overly broad, unduly burdensome, cumulative, and/or duplicative to the extent it seeks documents or records that are not within the current knowledge, possession, custody, or control of the Defendant. Plaintiff's request should be accessible to Plaintiff from Plaintiff's own files, from documents or information already in Plaintiff's possession. The Plaintiff did not attach a copy of the alleged contract and/or pertinent documents evidencing alleged charges to the Complaint [Fl.R.Civ.P. 1.130(a)], thus the probity of the requested information is speculative. The Defendant has sought the alleged contract, along with other alleged pertinent documents, on the account that is the subject matter of Plaintiff's Complaint through discovery and demands strict proof thereof.*

11. Identify by name and location, each and every document forwarded to Citibank objecting to any of the charges or advising the Plaintiff and/or Citibank of any set-offs.

*Objected to by Defendant on the grounds that it is overly broad, unduly burdensome, cumulative, and/or duplicative to the extent it seeks documents or records that are not within the current knowledge, possession, custody, or control of the Defendant. Plaintiff's request should be accessible to Plaintiff from Plaintiff's own files, from documents or information already in Plaintiff's possession. The Plaintiff did not attach a copy of the alleged contract and/or pertinent documents evidencing alleged charges to the Complaint [Fl.R.Civ.P. 1.130(a)], thus the probity of the requested information is speculative. The Defendant has sought the alleged contract, along with other alleged pertinent documents, on the account that is the subject matter of Plaintiff's Complaint through discovery and demands strict proof thereof.*

12. State the **full** name of each and every person who you believe acted on behalf of the Plaintiff, with which the Defendant

had any contacts regarding the subject matter of Plaintiff's claim or any defenses, set-offs or counter claims you have thereto.

*Objected to by Defendant to the extent that it is seeking information that is premature, given that the parties are in the midst of discovery and pertinent documents have not yet been produced by the Plaintiff. The Defendant cannot possibly answer this interrogatory when she has not seen the Plaintiff's answers to her discovery.*

*Without waiving her objection, the Defendant, upon completion of discovery with the Plaintiff, will most definitely have defenses in this action and will provide such defenses to the Plaintiff if asked through discovery. The Defendant reserves the right to update this answer to this interrogatory at a later time when that decision is made.*

13.     Set forth the factual basis for each and every defense and/or counter claim you asset against Plaintiff's claim.

*Objected to by Defendant to the extent that it is seeking information that is premature, given that the parties are in the midst of discovery and pertinent documents have not yet been produced by the Plaintiff. The Defendant cannot possibly answer this interrogatory when she has not seen the Plaintiff's answers to her discovery.*

*Without waiving her objection, the Defendant, upon completion of discovery with the Plaintiff, will most definitely have defenses in this action and will provide such defenses to the Plaintiff if asked through discovery. The Defendant reserves the right to update this answer to this interrogatory at a later time when that decision is made.*

**Note:** This document was signed by me and notarized.

IN THE COUNTY COURT IN AND FOR POLK COUNTY, FLORIDA
CIVIL DIVISION

ASSET ACCEPTANCE, LLC

      Plaintiff

vs.                          Case No. 5311CC1415

SHEILA R. MUNOZ,

      Defendant

## NOTICE OF SERVICE OF
## ANSWER TO REQUEST FOR ADMISSIONS

YOU ARE NOTIFIED that the undersigned has served Answers to Request for Admissions to Plaintiff, Asset Acceptance, LLC, on this 9th day of June, 2011, by First Class Mail.

## CERTIFICATE OF SERVICE

I HEREBY CERTIFY that a true and correct copy of the foregoing was mailed to Plaintiff's attorney this 9th day of June, 2011, to the following address:

Amanda R. Duffy
Asset Acceptance, LLC
PO Box 9065
Brandon, FL 33509

SHEILA R. MUNOZ, Defendant

# PLAINTIFF'S REQUEST
# FOR ADMISSIONS TO DEFENDANT

Plaintiff, Asset Acceptance, LLC, by and through its undersigned attorney, pursuant to Fl.R.Civ.P. 1.370, demands that Defendant, Sheila R. Munoz, admits or denies the truth of the following statements within thirty (30) days of this request. Fl.R.Civ.P. 1.370 directs that the matters asserted herein shall be admitted for the purposes of summary judgment or trial unless you serve a written answer or objection addressed to the matter within 30 days after service of the request.

1.      That this is an action for damages that is within the court's jurisdiction, exclusive of interest and court costs.

*Defendant states that after a reasonable inquiry, the information known or readily obtainable by her is insufficient to enable her to admit or deny this request.*

2.      That the Defendant is a resident of XXXX, FL.

*Admits*

3.      That the Defendant applied for a Citibank credit card.

*Defendant states that after a reasonable inquiry, the information known or readily obtainable by her is insufficient to enable her to admit or deny this request.*

4.      That the Defendant opened a Citibank credit card account with Citibank on November 26, 2004.

*Defendant states that after a reasonable inquiry, the information known or readily obtainable by her is insufficient to enable her to admit or deny this request.*

5.      That the Defendant received a Citibank card member agreement.

*Defendant states that after a reasonable inquiry, the information known or readily obtainable by her is insufficient to enable her to admit or deny this request.*

6.      That the terms of the Citibank card member agreement govern the relationship between Defendant, Sheila R. Munoz, and Citibank with respect to merchandise and services purchased on the Citibank credit card account that is the subject of the Plaintiff's Complaint.

*Defendant states that after a reasonable inquiry, the information known or readily obtainable by her is insufficient to enable her to admit or deny this request.*

7.      That the Defendant used the Citibank credit card account that is the subject of Plaintiff's Complaint to purchase merchandise and services.

*Defendant states that after a reasonable inquiry, the information known or readily obtainable by her is insufficient to enable her to admit or deny this request.*

8.      That the Defendant received credit card services from Citibank.

*Defendant states that after a reasonable inquiry, the information known or readily obtainable by her is insufficient to enable her to admit or deny this request.*

9.      The Defendant accepted the benefits of the credit card in accordance with the terms and conditions of the credit card agreement.

*Defendant states that after a reasonable inquiry, the information known or readily obtainable by her is insufficient to enable her to admit or deny this request.*

10.     That the Defendant made payments to Citibank.

*Defendant states that after a reasonable inquiry, the information known or readily obtainable by her is insufficient to enable her to admit or deny this request.*

11.      That the Defendant failed to make payment on the Citibank account that is the subject of the Plaintiff's Complaint since Defendant made a partial payment on or about April 30, 2007.

*Defendant states that after a reasonable inquiry, the information known or readily obtainable by her is insufficient to enable her to admit or deny this request.*

12.      That as a result of the Defendant's action, the Plaintiff has been damaged in the amounts of $13,171.06 in principal charges and $10,253.94 in interest charges.

*Defendant states that after a reasonable inquiry, the information known or readily obtainable by her is insufficient to enable her to admit or deny this request.*

13.      That the Defendant received statements from Citibank reflecting the balance due on the account that is the subject of the Plaintiff's Complaint.

*Defendant states that after a reasonable inquiry, the information known or readily obtainable by her is insufficient to enable her to admit or deny this request.*

14.      That the Defendant failed to object to statements itemizing purchases and reflecting the balance due on the account that is the subject of the Plaintiff's Complaint.

*Defendant states that after a reasonable inquiry, the information known or readily obtainable by her is insufficient to enable her to admit or deny this request.*

15.      The Defendant owes the Plaintiff the charge off amount of $13,171.06 in principal and $10,253.94 in interest.

*Defendant states that after a reasonable inquiry, the information known or readily obtainable by her is insufficient to enable her to admit or deny this request.*

IN THE COUNTY COURT IN AND FOR POLK COUNTY, FLORIDA
CIVIL DIVISION

ASSET ACCEPTANCE, LLC

      Plaintiff

vs.                          Case No. 5311CC1415

SHEILA R. MUNOZ,

      Defendant

## NOTICE OF SERVICE OF ANSWER TO REQUEST FOR PRODUCTION OF DOCUMENTS

YOU ARE NOTIFIED that the undersigned has served Answers to Request for Production of Documents to Plaintiff, Asset Acceptance, LLC, on this 9th day of June, 2011, by First Class Mail.

## CERTIFICATE OF SERVICE

I HEREBY CERTIFY that a true and correct copy of the foregoing was mailed to Plaintiff's attorney this 9th day of June, 2011, to the following address:

Amanda R. Duffy
Asset Acceptance, LLC
PO Box 9065
Brandon, FL 33509

SHEILA R. MUNOZ, Defendant

# PLAINTIFF'S REQUEST
# FOR PRODUCTION OF DOCUMENTS

Plaintiff, Asset Acceptance, LLC, by and through its undersigned attorney, pursuant to Fl.R.Civ.P. 1.350, requests that Defendant, Sheila R. Munoz, produce at the offices of Asset Acceptance, LLC, P.O. Box 9065, Brandon, FL 33509, the following documents within thirty (30) days of service of this request.

## ITEMS TO BE PRODUCED

1.     Any and all documents relating to the indebtedness that is the subject matter of the Plaintiff's Complaint.

*Defendant objects to the Plaintiff's request for Documents No. 1 as it assumes there is an account being sued upon where no account has been identified as of yet by the Plaintiff or its attorneys. It is burdensome to the extent it seeks documents or records that are not within the current knowledge, possession, custody, or control of the Defendant, more readily accessible to Plaintiff from Plaintiff's own files, from documents or information already in Plaintiff's possession. Defendant cannot provide what is requested.*

2.     Any and all documents relating to any set-offs, counter claims, or complaints regarding the credit card purchases and cash advances that are the subject matter of the Plaintiff's Complaint.

*Defendant objects to the Plaintiff's request for Documents No. 2 as it assumes there is an account being sued upon where no account has been identified as of yet by the Plaintiff or its attorneys. It is burdensome to the extent it seeks documents or records that are not within the current knowledge, possession, custody, or control of the Defendant, more readily accessible to Plaintiff from Plaintiff's own files, from documents or information already in Plaintiff's possession. Defendant cannot provide what is requested.*

3.     Any and all documents you intend to offer or proffer into evidence into this cause.

*Defendant objects to the Plaintiff's request for Documents No. 3 as it is requesting information that is premature, given that the parties are in the midst of discovery, and pertinent documents have not yet been produced by the Plaintiff. Without waiving her objection, the Defendant at this time has no documents to offer into evidence, but reserves the right to offer documents, if need be, once the Plaintiff answers the discovery given by the Defendant.*

4.      Any and all credit applications and guarantees submitted or delivered to Citibank by Defendant.

*Defendant objects to the Plaintiff's request for Documents No. 4 as it assumes there is an account being sued upon where no account has been identified as of yet by the Plaintiff or its attorneys. It is burdensome to the extent it seeks documents or records that are not within the current knowledge, possession, custody, or control of the Defendant, more readily accessible to Plaintiff from Plaintiff's own files, from documents or information already in Plaintiff's possession. Defendant cannot provide what is requested.*

5.      Any and all correspondence mailed by the Defendant to Citibank or Plaintiff indicating any dispute as to the account that is the subject matter of Plaintiff's Complaint.

*Defendant objects to the Plaintiff's request for Documents No. 5 as it assumes there is an account being sued upon where no account has been identified as of yet by the Plaintiff or its attorneys. It is burdensome to the extent it seeks documents or records that are not within the current knowledge, possession, custody, or control of the Defendant, more readily accessible to Plaintiff from Plaintiff's own files, from documents or information already in Plaintiff's possession. Defendant cannot provide what is requested.*

6.      Any and all bills or statements received by Defendant itemizing purchases made and balance due on the account that is the subject matter of the Plaintiff's Complaint.

*Defendant objects to the Plaintiff's request for Documents No. 6 as it assumes there is an account being sued upon where no account has been identified as of yet by the Plaintiff or its attorneys. It is burdensome to the extent it seeks documents or records that are not within the current knowledge, possession, custody, or control of the Defendant, more readily accessible to Plaintiff from*

*Plaintiff's own files, from documents or information already in Plaintiff's possession. Defendant cannot provide what is requested.*

7.      Any and all documents evidencing payments made by Defendant on the account that is the subject matter of Plaintiff's Complaint.

*Defendant objects to the Plaintiff's request for Documents No. 7 as it assumes there is an account being sued upon where no account has been identified as of yet by the Plaintiff or its attorneys. It is burdensome to the extent it seeks documents or records that are not within the current knowledge, possession, custody, or control of the Defendant, more readily accessible to Plaintiff from Plaintiff's own files, from documents or information already in Plaintiff's possession. Defendant cannot provide what is requested.*

8.      Any and all documents forwarded by Defendant to Citibank or regarding the Defendant's Citibank account.

*Defendant objects to the Plaintiff's request for Documents No. 8 as it assumes there is an account being sued upon where no account has been identified as of yet by the Plaintiff or its attorneys. It is burdensome to the extent it seeks documents or records that are not within the current knowledge, possession, custody, or control of the Defendant, more readily accessible to Plaintiff from Plaintiff's own files, from documents or information already in Plaintiff's possession. Defendant cannot provide what is requested.*

# Chapter 4

# Three Motions To Strike, Sworn Denial, and Additional Affirmative Defenses

***Note:*** The actual Motion To Strike Bill of Sale and Assignment, the Motion To Strike Card Agreement, the Motion To Strike Affidavit, the Sworn Denial, and Additional Affirmative Defenses used in this case may be found at the end of this chapter.

This is another place where a consumer must rely on their state's or the Federal Rules of Civil Procedure. Each state is different.

In my case, after looking over the "evidence" that was attached to the Summons and Complaint and finding glaring problems, I decided to file a Motion To Strike for each document, the Bill of Sale and Assignment, the Card Agreement, and the Affidavit. My thinking was that if any of the motions were upheld, that whittled away at Asset Acceptance, LLC's, case against me. If all three motions were upheld, the case would have no cause of action.

In fact, in Florida and many other states (Rules of Civil Procedure), the basis of the Complaint must be attached to the Complaint. For example, when one looks at Asset Acceptance, LLC's, Complaint, the first count is "Breach of Contract." What contract? There was no original contract attached to the Complaint. The Florida Rules of Civil Procedure require the bonds, notes, bills of exchange, contracts, accounts, or documents upon which action may be brought to be attached. Right there is an affirmative defense.

So, I filed a Motion To Strike against each of the three documents individually.

In addition I filed a Sworn Denial. The Sworn Denial countered the Affidavit attached to the Complaint, thereby forcing Asset Acceptance, LLC, to have to produce a live witness to testify at the trial and submitting to cross examination regarding the Affidavit. I wondered how Crystal Janus would testify as to the Affidavit and its authenticity.

These documents may be found at the end of this chapter. It is important to note that each of these documents had attached to it a "Certificate of Service." One copy would be retained by the consumer for personal records; one would be filed with the court; one would be mailed to the attorney of the JDB.

Discovery also revealed many more Affirmative Defenses that I decided I could use. I made a list of these as "Additional Affirmative Defenses" possibly to be used in a future Motion To Dismiss, Motion for Summary Judgment, or, in the event the case went all the way to trial, at the trial itself. I filed the list with the court and sent a copy to Amanda Duffy, Asset Acceptance LLC's, in-house attorney, so that it would be a matter of record before the case went to trial, in the event the case made it that far. This document may be found at the end of this chapter.

IN THE COUNTY COURT IN AND FOR POLK COUNTY, FLORIDA
CIVIL DIVISION

ASSET ACCEPTANCE, LLC

     Plaintiff

vs.                          Case No. 5311CC1415

SHEILA R. MUNOZ,

     Defendant


**MOTION TO STRIKE BILL OF SALE AND ASSIGNMENT**

Comes now, Defendant Sheila R. Munoz, PRO SE, and respectfully states the following:

1.     Plaintiff has submitted into evidence a BILL OF SALE AND ASSIGNMENT.

2.     Plaintiff has not provided a PURCHASE AND SALE AGREEMENT to support the terms and conditions under which the alleged sale of the account was done. The record does not disclose this information, and it cannot be assumed without creating an unfair prejudice against the Defendant.

3.     The Bill of Sale and Assignment does not reference the Defendant's name or account number with Citibank. The Bill of Sale and Assignment could be referencing anyone's account and in no way proves that it is referencing the Defendant or her account. In *Unifund CCR Partners v. Cavender*, No. 2007-CC-3040, 14 Fla.L. Weekly Supp. 975b (Orange Cty, July 20, 2007), the court held that a debt buyer "assignment" that does not refer to specific accounts does not establish ownership by the Plaintiff, nor is testimony based on a computer screen sufficient: "The Court has reviewed the documents presented by the Plaintiff, Bill of Sale and the Assignment, and finds that they fail to sufficiently identify the accounts that were assigned or sold to the Plaintiff. Neither the Bill

of Sale nor the Assignment indicate the account numbers or names of account holders. They do not provide any information that would allow the Court to determine if the alleged account of Defendant was one of the accounts sold or assigned to the Plaintiff. Without any indicia of ownership that would sufficiently identify the true owner of the account at the time that Plaintiff filed this action, the Plaintiff is unable to prove that it had standing to bring the action. An assignment is the basis of the Plaintiff's standing to invoke the processes of the Court in the first place and is, therefore, an essential element of proof. . . ."

4.    The Bill of Sale and Assignment is not authenticated (notarized or certified as true copies of the originals). *Citibank (South Dakota), NA. v. Martin*, 11 Misc. 3d 219; 807 N.Y.S.2d 284 (Civ.Ct. 2005): ". . . as to assigned claims, it is essential that an assignee show its standing, which 'doctrine embraces several judicially self-imposed limits on the exercise of . . . jurisdiction, such as the general prohibition on a litigant's raising another person's legal rights.' . . . A lack of standing renders the litigation a nullity, subject to dismissal without prejudice. . . . It is the assignee's burden to prove the assignment. . . . Given that courts are reluctant to credit a naked conclusory affidavit on a matter exclusively within a moving party's knowledge . . . an assignee must tender proof of assignment of a particular account or, if there were an oral assignment, evidence of consideration paid and delivery of the assignment. . . ."

5.    The Bill of Sale and Assignment is vague and does not prove that the said account was ever assigned from Citibank to the Plaintiff.

WHEREFORE, the Defendant prays this Honorable Court that Plaintiff's Bill of Sale and Assignment be stricken from evidence in the above action.

I state under penalty of perjury that the foregoing is true and correct.

 5/10/2011
_____
Sheila R. Munoz, Defendant

## CERTIFICATE OF SERVICE

I HEREBY CERTIFY that a true and correct copy of the foregoing was mailed to Plaintiff's attorney this 10th day of May, 2011, to the following address:

Amanda R. Duffy
Asset Acceptance, LLC
PO Box 9065
Brandon, FL 33509

SHEILA R. MUNOZ, Defendant

IN THE COUNTY COURT IN AND FOR POLK COUNTY, FLORIDA
CIVIL DIVISION

ASSET ACCEPTANCE, LLC

       Plaintiff

vs.                            Case No. 5311CC1415

SHEILA R. MUNOZ,

       Defendant

## MOTION TO STRIKE CARD AGREEMENT

Comes now, Defendant Sheila R. Munoz, PRO SE, and respectfully states the following:

1.      Plaintiff has submitted into evidence a CARD AGREEMENT.

2.      The Credit Card Agreement lacks the Defendant's signature and date or account number or other identifying statements that connect it to the Defendant. In *MBNA America Bank, NA. v. Nelson*, 13777/06, 2007 NY Slip Op 51200U; 2007 N.Y. Misc. LEXIS 4317 (N.Y. Civ. Ct. May 24, 2007), the credit card issuer must tender the actual provisions agreed to, including any and all amendments, and not simply a photocopy of general terms to which the credit issuer may currently demand debtors agree. See *MBNA America Bank, NA v. Nelson,* supra.

3.      Plaintiff states the alleged account was opened in 2004. The date on the last page of the Credit Card Agreement shows 2006.

WHEREFORE, the Defendant prays this Honorable Court that Plaintiff's Card Agreement be stricken from evidence in the above action.

I state under penalty of perjury that the foregoing is true and correct.

 5/10/2011
Sheila R. Munoz, Defendant

## CERTIFICATE OF SERVICE

I HEREBY CERTIFY that a true and correct copy of the foregoing was mailed to Plaintiff's attorney this 10th day of May, 2011, to the following address:

Amanda R. Duffy
Asset Acceptance, LLC
PO Box 9065
Brandon, FL 33509

SHEILA R. MUNOZ, Defendant

# IN THE COUNTY COURT IN AND FOR POLK COUNTY, FLORIDA
## CIVIL DIVISION

ASSET ACCEPTANCE, LLC

      Plaintiff

vs.                            Case No. 5311CC1415

SHEILA R. MUNOZ,

      Defendant

## MOTION TO STRIKE AFFIDAVIT

Comes now, Defendant Sheila R. Munoz, PRO SE, and respectfully states the following:

1.      Plaintiff has submitted into evidence an AFFIDAVIT.

2.      Plaintiff has not provided a PURCHASE AND SALE AGREEMENT to support the terms and conditions under which the alleged sale of the account was done. The record does not disclose this information, and it cannot be assumed without creating an unfair prejudice against the Defendant.

3.      Said Affidavit pertains to acts and events that allegedly occurred between Defendant and a third party, Citibank.

4.      At no time was the creator of the Affidavit or any of Plaintiff's employees present to witness any alleged acts or creation of the records of transactions occurring between Defendant and Citibank.

5.      As such, said Affidavit falls under the hearsay rule and is inadmissible as evidence, pursuant to FS 90.801(1)(c) and FS 90.802.

6.      The information contained in the Affidavit is merely an accumulation of hearsay; and,

7.     Upon information and belief, the creator of the document is not currently and has never been employed with Citibank and, therefore, cannot have personal knowledge of how Citibank records were prepared and maintained (i.e., chain of custody).

8.     An affidavit must clearly show the affiant is competent to testify to the matters stated in the affidavit. Fl.R.Civ.P. 1.510 Author's Comment -- 1967 [hereinafter "FRCP 1.510 Comment"]; *Elser v. Law Offices of James M. Russ, P.A.*, 679 So. 2d 309 (Fla. 5th DCA 1996). An affiant fails to satisfy this competency requirement where affiant merely states, without more, that affiant has "personal knowledge." Id.; see also *Montejo Invests, N.V. v. Green Cos., Inc. of Fla.*, 471 So 2d 158 (Fla. 3d DCA 1985) where affiant merely stated his title, that he was familiar with the facts stated in the complaint, and that to the best of his knowledge and belief the facts were true and accurate, affidavit was legally insufficient as it failed to show affirmatively that affiant was competent to testify to matters set forth therein, was not based on personal knowledge, and did not set forth facts as would be admissible in evidence; *Iglesia v. City of Miami Beach*, 487 So. 2d 1205 (Fla. 3d DCA 1986), rev. denied, 494 So. 2d 1151 (Fla. 1986) "addition of the phrase that the affiant is 'personally knowledgeable' with respect to the allegations of the complaint adds nothing, since it is not a statement of fact, but is itself a mere conclusion or opinion of the affiant." An affiant should establish the factual basis for affiant's competence (i.e., age, bases of affiant's personal knowledge of the relevant matters at issue in the case, etc.) M. Tanner & E. Gonzalez, Florida Civil Trial Preparation, Motion Practice (Fla.. Bar 2002). Therefore, the affiant is unqualified to testify as to the truth of the information contained in the Affidavit.

WHEREFORE, the Defendant prays this Honorable Court that Plaintiff's Affidavit be stricken from evidence in the above action.

I state under penalty of perjury that the foregoing is true and correct.

███████████  5/10/2011
Sheila R. Munoz, Defendant

## CERTIFICATE OF SERVICE

I HEREBY CERTIFY that a true and correct copy of the foregoing was mailed to Plaintiff's attorney this 10th day of May, 2011, to the following address:

Amanda R. Duffy
Asset Acceptance, LLC
PO Box 9065
Brandon, FL 33509

███████████████

SHEILA R. MUNOZ, Defendant

████████████████████

# IN THE COUNTY COURT IN AND FOR POLK COUNTY, FLORIDA
## CIVIL DIVISION

ASSET ACCEPTANCE, LLC

     Plaintiff

vs.                            Case No. 5311CC1415

SHEILA R. MUNOZ,

     Defendant

## SWORN DENIAL

I, Sheila R. Munoz, deny this is my debt, and if it is my debt, I deny that it is still a valid debt; and if it is a valid debt, I deny the amount sued for is the correct amount.

 5/10/2011
Sheila R. Munoz, Defendant

STATE OF FLORIDA

COUNTY OF POLK

BEFORE ME, the undersigned authority, personally appeared Sheila R. Munoz, who being by me first duly sworn, deposes and says that she executed the foregoing Sworn Denial and that it is true and correct to the best of her knowledge and belief.

Notary Public, State of Florida
Type of ID produced: FL Driver's License
My Commission Expires:

# CERTIFICATE OF SERVICE

I HEREBY CERTIFY that a true and correct copy of the foregoing was mailed to Plaintiff's attorney this 10th day of May, 2011, to the following address:

Amanda R. Duffy
Asset Acceptance, LLC
PO Box 9065
Brandon, FL 33509

---
SHEILA R. MUNOZ, Defendant

> **Note:** It would have been better if I had included as many of these Affirmative Defenses in my original Answer to the Summons and Complaint. However, many of these defenses I was unaware of at the time I answered the Summons and Complaint, and some were not forthcoming until after discovery.

IN THE COUNTY COURT IN AND FOR POLK COUNTY, FLORIDA
CIVIL DIVISION

ASSET ACCEPTANCE, LLC

     Plaintiff

vs.                                               Case No. 5311CC1415

SHEILA R. MUNOZ,

     Defendant

## ADDITIONAL AFFIRMATIVE DEFENSES
## AFTER DISCOVERY

1.     Defendant re-alleges the Affirmative Defenses given within the Answer to Complaint and Summons set forth in paragraphs 1-22 as if fully set forth herein.

2.     Defendant has disputed and continues to dispute the alleged debt asserted by the Plaintiff in this claim.

3.     "Implicit in the right to self-representation is the obligation on the part of the Court to make reasonable allowances to protect pro se litigants from inadvertent forfeiture of important rights because of their lack of legal training." And "the Court's duty is even broader in the case of a pro se defendant who finds himself in court against his will with little time to learn the intricacies of civil procedure and law." See 28 U.S.C.A. 1654.

4.     For most civil claims, a Plaintiff must present a **prima facie case** to avoid dismissal of the case or an unfavorable directed verdict. The Plaintiff must produce enough evidence on all elements of the claim to support the claim and shift the burden of evidence production to the Defendant. If the Plaintiff fails to make a prima facie case, the Defendant may move for dismissal or a favorable directed verdict without presenting any evidence to rebut whatever evidence the Plaintiff has presented. This is because the burden of persuading a judge or jury always rests with the Plaintiff.

To that regard, the Plaintiff's alleged "Bill of Sale and Assignment" indicates the Plaintiff received from the original creditor "the Accounts listed in Exhibit 1 and the final electronic file." However, on August 9, 2011, the Plaintiff issued a Subpoena Duces Tecum to the original creditor commanding them to turn over all the documents pertaining to the alleged debt, which indicates misrepresenting the debt they allege the Defendant owes.

5.     **Failure to Notify:** Plaintiff did not provide Defendant a written notice of any assignment between Citibank and Asset Acceptance, LLC, within 30 days after the assignment. (FDCPA 559.715) In Discovery, Plaintiff provided a copy of such a letter, which is dated August 9, 2010, 41 days after the date of June 29, 2010, which is the date the alleged purchase of the debt occurred. Defendant also certifies she never received such letter.

**"Florida State Statute Regulating Debt Collection/Debt Collectors, Title 33, PART VI. CONSUMER COLLECTION PRACTICES**
**559.715 Assignment of consumer debts.**--This part does not prohibit the assignment, by a creditor, of the right to bill and collect a consumer debt. However, the assignee must give the debtor written notice of such assignment within 30 days after the assignment. The assignee is a real party in interest and may bring an action in a court of competent jurisdiction to collect a debt that has been assigned to such assignee and is in default."

The Plaintiff failed to meet the deadline for presentation of their answers to discovery by the Defendant by **12 days**, and the Plaintiff failed to give the Defendant 30-day notice of the purchase and assignment of the alleged debt by **11 days**. Asset Acceptance, LLC, was founded in 1962 "for the purpose of purchasing and collecting charged-off consumer receivables" (Asset Acceptance, LLC, website). They most certainly would know the law as it pertains to deadlines for Notice to the Debtor of their purchase and assignment of a debt, as well as the time allotment for timely answers to a discovery. Their behavior portrays their blatant disregard to the law as it pertains to timeframes stipulated by law.

6.      Plaintiff has failed to provide a detailed list of the debts to the Defendant in the initial debt collection notice as required by the FDCPA and as evidenced by case law: *Coppola v. Arrow Financial Services*, 302CV577, 2002 WL 32173704 (D.Conn., Oct. 29, 2002).

Although this was requested in discovery, Plaintiff failed to provide.

7.      **Doctrines of Scienti et volenti non fit injuria** (a person who knowledgeably consents to legal wrong has no legal right) and **Damnum absque injuria** (harm without injury).

8.      **Unclean Hands:** Plaintiff has concealed Defendant's rights under the alleged "Card Agreement" that was attached to the Summons of the Defendant's legal arbitration right to waive Plaintiff from this court venue.

9.      Plaintiff failed to name the real party in interest [Fl.R.Civ.P. Rule 1.210(a)]. The alleged "Purchase and Sale Agreement" attached to Plaintiff's Complaint does not show the terms and conditions under which the purchase of the debt was done or whether or not the purported assignment was partial or complete.

In *Munoz v. Pipestone Financial, LLC*, 397 F.Supp.2nd 1129 (D. Minn. 2005) the court determined that the language "all rights, title and interest of Seller in and to those certain receivables, judgments or evidences of debt" when used in connection with an assignment of credit card accounts did not permit the assignee to collect interest or attorneys' fees on the accounts based on the user agreement and its language. Id., 397 F. Supp.2nd at 1131-32.

Without knowing the terms of the sale and/or assignment, Plaintiff also fails to acknowledge that the Assignor even has knowledge of the action or whether all rights and control or only partial were given to the Plaintiff and without this information, it cannot be assumed without creating an unfair prejudice against the Defendant.

Although this information was requested in discovery, Plaintiff did not provide.

10.    **Lack of Standing -- No Proof of Account:** The affidavit that was attached to Plaintiff's Complaint had a signature that was notarized, but the notary did not reveal the proof of identification of the signer. The Defendant researched diligently as to a person named "Crystal Janus" only to find two in the nation, both of whom live in Monroe, Michigan. This document has all the earmarks of being "robosigned" by a false identity.

The original Credit Card Application with Defendant's signature or electronic signature, proof of debt, receipts, purchases and/or cash advances, payments, third party payments, statements, etc., were not attached.

Although these were requested in discovery, Plaintiff failed to provide.

11.    **Lack of Standing -- No Proof of Ownership:** Plaintiff has failed to prove ownership of the alleged debt and, therefore, has failed to prove the legal standing to sue. The signatures on the "Bill of Sale and Assignment" were not dated nor notarized, failing to verify the real identity of those signing or when they signed. This document has the earmarks of being "robosigned."

12.    Plaintiff voluntarily, **with prior knowledge inherent of possible risk**, assumed ownership of a purported debt and is not entitled to judgment and not entitled to equitable, pecuniary, or statutory damages. Any damages to Plaintiff were self-induced; therefore, the Plaintiff is barred from seeking relief for damages.

13.    **Lack of Privity:** Defendant has never entered into any contractual or debtor/creditor arrangements with the Plaintiff.

14.    **Lack of Cause of Action:** "A complaint based on a written instrument does not state a cause of action until the instrument,

or an adequate portion thereof, is attached to or incorporated in the complaint." *Samuels v. King Motor Co. of Ft. Lauderdale*, 782 So.2d 489 (Fla. App. 4 Dist. 1992); see also *Contractors Unlimited, Inc. v. Nortrax Equipment Co. Southeast*, 833 So.2d 286 (Fla. 5th DCA 2002).

15. **Plaintiff failed to state a claim upon which relief can be granted.** Plaintiff failed to state facts/laws sufficient to constitute cause of action against the Defendant upon which relief can be granted.

16. **Plaintiff violated Statute of Frauds:** The purported Card Agreement falls within a class of contracts or agreements required to be in writing. The purported agreement alleged in the Complaint is not in writing and signed by the Defendant or by some other person authorized by the Defendant, and who was to answer for the alleged debt, default, or miscarriage of another person.

17. **Doctrine of Laches:** The Plaintiff or the person or entity that assigned the alleged claim to the Plaintiff waited too long to file this lawsuit, making it difficult or impossible for any Defendant to find possible witnesses or possible evidence necessary to provide a defense for a Defendant or that possible evidence necessary to provide for a Defendant's defense would have been lost or destroyed.

18. Defendant alleges that the Complaint includes references to alleged agreements made outside of the purported written contract, violating the Parol Evidence Rule.

19. Plaintiff is barred under Fair Debt Collection Practices Act 807(2), 15 U.S.C. 1692e(2) from collecting interest on any amount unless it is expressly authorized by the agreement creating a debt or permitted by law. No credit card application with Defendant's signature or electronic signature showing terms of the account was attached to Plaintiff's Complaint. Also, it has not been established that the Plaintiff even owns this debt.

Although this information was requested in discovery, Plaintiff failed to provide.

20.    **Accord and Satisfaction:** Original creditor accepted payment from a third party for the purported debt or a portion of the purported debt or received other compensation in the form of monies or credits from the Plaintiff. If an original creditor accepts any payment on the alleged debt by a third party, it makes a new contract for which Defendant is not liable.

The terms and amount of this "value received" as referred to in the purported "Bill of Sale and Assignment" was requested in discovery, but Plaintiff failed to provide.

21.    Any damages to Plaintiff are the result of acts or omissions committed by non-parties to this action, over whom Defendant has no responsibility or control.

22.    **Failure of Consideration:** No exchange of money or goods occurred between Plaintiff and Defendant.

23.    **Unjust Enrichment:** Granting of the Plaintiff's demand by the Court would result in Unjust Enrichment, as Plaintiff would receive more money than Plaintiff is entitled to receive.

24.    Since a Court will not grant a judgment or other legal relief to a party who has not acted fairly by having made false representations or concealing material facts from the other part, Defendant maintains that **equitable estoppel** bars Plaintiff's claims.

25.    **Defendant is Execution-Proof** as it relates to a possible judgment: Defendant is "Head of Household": Defendant is the caregiver in Defendant's home of an adult daughter who is permanently and totally disabled with a terminal disease. Defendant provides 50% or more of her support. Head of Household income is exempt from attachment.

Defendant's husband is also permanently and totally disabled, with his sole income being from SSD, which money is deposited in their bank account with a normal balance of less than his monthly income, which exempts the bank account from attachment.

Defendant's home has a Homestead Exemption, which exempts it from a judgment lien or attachment.

Defendant has no other assets to which a judgment could be attached.

26. Defendant reserves the right to plead additional Affirmative Defenses as become applicable and/or available at a later time.

SHEILA R. MUNOZ, Defendant

## CERTIFICATE OF SERVICE

I HEREBY CERTIFY that a true and correct copy of the foregoing was mailed to Plaintiff's attorney this 27th day of June, 2011, to the following address:

Amanda R. Duffy
Asset Acceptance, LLC
PO Box 9065
Brandon, FL 33509

SHEILA R. MUNOZ, Defendant

# Chapter 5

# The Counterclaim, Motion To Dismiss, Motion To Compel, and Motion for Summary Judgment with Prejudice

**Note:** The actual Counterclaim, Motion To Dismiss, Motion To Compel, and Motion for Summary Judgment with Prejudice used in my case may be found at the end of this chapter. Exhibits (evidence) referred to in these documents are not included, as they are specific to this case only. However, one would attach their own Exhibits to documents as needed and clearly identify them, as well as reference them within the motion/counterclaim as shown in the examples.

At this point in my case, I was somewhat satisfied with Discovery. Not all of my questions had been answered, but I believed I had enough ammunition to go up against Asset Acceptance, LLC. My confidence was increasing. There were still my three Motions To Strike that needed to be heard by the judge, but I felt confident since Amanda Duffy, Asset Acceptance, LLC's, in-house attorney, had not filed any objections to any of them.

If I found I needed the answers to any unanswered questions or a partially answered question, I still had the option to file a Motion To Compel, requesting the court to order Asset Acceptance, LLC, to respond.

Even after Discovery seems to be wrapped up, if either side realizes they need to ask additional interrogatories or request additional documents to be produced or wants to submit additional admissions, the Rules of Civil Procedure must be referred to again. In the state of Florida, as long as one does not exceed the limit in the number of questions asked, a consumer may send further Discovery.

Now that Discovery seemed to be finished, I had several issues on which to base a counterclaim. Here is one area in which I erred, in that since I had not included a counterclaim along with my Answer to the Summons and Complaint and Affirmative Defenses, according to the Florida Rules of Civil Procedure, I should have asked leave (permission) of the court to file a counterclaim. Asking leave of court is done in the form of a motion. I did not do that. It could have been a costly mistake.

Without asking leave of court to do so, I drafted a counterclaim and filed it with the court, along with the Certificate of Service. I kept a copy for myself, and mailed a copy to Amanda Duffy, Asset Acceptance, LLC's, in-house attorney, along with the Certificate of Service. This document may be found at the end of this chapter.

A counterclaim is an actual lawsuit against the JDB. Therefore, the JDB's attorney must answer it in the same manner as the lawsuit that was served on the consumer. It is actually two lawsuits flowing side by side. In my case, Amanda Duffy, Asset Acceptance, LLC's, in-house attorney, had 20 days plus an additional five days for mailing to answer my counterclaim, just as I originally had to answer Asset Acceptance, LLC's Summons and Complaint against me.

There was enough evidence in my case at this point that I believed I could move for a dismissal of Asset Acceptance, LLC's, case against me with prejudice. Therefore, on the same day I filed the counterclaim with the court, I filed a Motion To Dismiss with prejudice. I remembered to add the Certificate of Service and to send a copy to Amanda Duffy, Asset Acceptance, LLC's, in-house attorney. This document may be found at the end of this chapter.

The 20-day deadline to receive an Answer to my counterclaim came and went. In fact, I even waited an additional 10 days to be sure. Still, no answer from Asset Acceptance, LLC, on the counterclaim. I could now file a Motion for (Default) Summary Judgment.

Remember how 90% of Defendants of JDB lawsuits never answer their Summons and Complaint and, therefore, are given a Default Summary Judgment? The same is true in reverse against the JDB. A default judgment may be placed on the JDB for not answering a Summons and Complaint from the consumer just as a default judgment may be placed on a consumer for not answering a Summons and Complaint from a JDB.

The Motion for Summary Judgment had more teeth in it: I was also asking for statutory damages (those specified by law), actual damages (actual expenses I incurred in my defense), and punitive damages (fines in order to punish an entity so that, hopefully, they would not repeat the offense).

When Asset Acceptance, LLC, received my Motion for Summary Judgment with Prejudice, Amanda Duffy called me. The first words out of her mouth were, "Well, you certainly got our attention. What can we do to settle this?"

That was music to my ears. Finally a response! I could barely believe I actually seemed to be winning my case – and all without the aid of an attorney. I was now in the driver's seat.

Having an attorney would have saved me a lot of time, stress, and worry, but I had been unable to find one who wanted to actually fight a lawsuit. All the lawyers I spoke with, trying to find legal help (in excess of 15 in all), seemed to fit into two distinct categories: those who wanted me to file bankruptcy to the tune of $1,200-$1,500 and those who only wanted to sue for FDCPA violations alone for a quick open-shut case in which I would receive $100-$1,000 total, but the attorney could easily receive $3,500 or more in attorney fees. I knew my case had traveled deeper than that, especially in light of the fact that this case was costing me hundreds of hours of not being with my terminally ill daughter physically, mentally, and emotionally.

I asked Amanda Duffy, Asset Acceptance, LLC's, in-house attorney, "What do you have to offer to settle?"

Amanda said, "We will remove our tradeline from your credit report and dismiss the case with prejudice if you will drop all litigation."

I hesitated and then asked, "Is that all?" She replied a simple yes.

This could be a great place for a consumer to agree and walk away from any litigation in exchange for knowing the JDB would not come back another time to sue over the same debt and knowing the JDB would remove the negative tradeline from their credit report, which could improve their credit score. One could easily negotiate here for the JDB to also extinguish the debt, meaning they would not pass the debt back to the original creditor or sell it to another JDB. The debt would be extinguished, gone.

However, in this case, I believed the lawsuit had been drawn out unnecessarily and actually was illegal to file in the first place. Therefore, I preferred to continue with my counterclaim in the expectation of winning a monetary judgment.

At these junctures in a case, one must make a decision whether to walk away or pursue for monetary judgment, depending on their unique situation. No two cases are the same. One must carefully weigh the options and the possible outcomes of any options taken.

> **A Note on Settling:** No matter when or under what terms, one must be sure to always get the terms of settlement in writing. One needs to BE ABSOLUTELY SURE of what they are signing and to what they are agreeing.

As an example, sometimes a JDB will offer a consumer to settle for a partial payment of the debt, such as 25% or 30% off. What is not said is that the remainder will be sold to another JDB for collection or even given back to the original creditor for collection. And that is not to mention the statute of limitations resetting on the debt!

It may be in one's best interest to demand that the underlying debt be extinguished, never to be sold to another JDB or given back to the original creditor. The negative tradeline needs to be removed from the consumer's credit report. If the tradeline is not removed, it would remain on the credit report for seven years from the date of settlement. In addition, if the tradeline is not removed, the credit report may reflect that the consumer settled. If there are other debts in default, what message does that send them?

It would not hurt for one to get an attorney to advise them on the written agreement before signing it to be absolutely sure it is saying what they think it should say.

Almost another month passed. I waited to hear something on my Motion To Dismiss or my Motion for Summary Judgment. It had been almost five months since I had filed my first motion, and none of them had been heard by the judge. None of them had been answered or objected to by Asset Acceptance, LLC. Everything seemed to be hanging in the air. But why?

The Florida Rules of Civil Procedure do not address how to set a hearing on motions filed. However, a trial cannot proceed unless all motions have been heard. I realized if the motions were not heard, the case could eventually be dismissed for lack of prosecution. The case must continually be moving ahead, or the court will assume the consumer has lost interest and is no longer pursuing it. Asset Acceptance, LLC, did not file any objections to any motions filed by me, not even the Motion To Dismiss nor the Motion for Summary Judgment. I needed to do something to move this clog.

Calling the Clerk of Court's office to get clarification on how to get a hearing set, I was transferred to the Judge's Judicial Assistant (JA). The JA instructed me to contact Amanda Duffy, Asset Acceptance, LLC's, in-house attorney, by letter and/or phone to see if a hearing date could be agreed upon. A telephone call and a letter with cc: to the judge (copy at end of chapter) received no response. Therefore, I filed a Motion To Compel, requesting the court to compel Asset Acceptance, LLC, to coordinate a hearing date. The judge finally took it upon himself and set a date to hear all pending motions.

Amanda Duffy objected to the judge's selection of the date for the hearing as she had a class scheduled for that day. She requested the hearing be rescheduled. I objected to a rescheduling (copy of letter to judge at end of chapter), citing to the judge the continual delays and non-communication by Amanda Duffy during the lawsuit. The judge refused to reschedule the date.

Four days before the hearing, Asset Acceptance, LLC, scrambled and filed with the court objections to each motion that had been filed by me, except for the Motion To Dismiss, as well as an objection to the counterclaim.

When there was no objection to my Motion To Dismiss, I asked myself, "Why?" The fact that there was no objection to the Motion To Dismiss underlined Asset Acceptance, LLC's, desire at this time to get the case dropped. (Remember, Asset Acceptance, LLC, could voluntarily dismiss their case any time they wanted. But there would be a risk of a lawsuit against them by myself.)

Asset Acceptance, LLC's, objection to my counterclaim was based on the fact that I had not asked leave (permission) of the court to file the counterclaim, based on the Rules of Civil Procedure. Isn't it ironic that Asset Acceptance, LLC, wanted to enforce the Rules of Procedure when it was to their benefit, but when it is inconvenient for them to follow the Rules (requirement to attach the original credit card contract or statements to the "Breach of Contract" Complaint), they ignore them?

I went to the courthouse for the hearing on all pending motions. Amanda Duffy showed up, also. The hearing took place around a conference-style table with a court recorder to one side and a bailiff standing near the door. A judge sat at the head of the table.

The judge asked which motion should be heard first. Amanda Duffy piped up that she wanted the "Motion To Dismiss" to be heard first. Asset Acceptance, LLC, really wanted this case dropped. That was a clue to me. Therefore, I stated I wanted to drop the Motion To Dismiss. Amanda Duffy appeared astounded.

The judge asked me which motion I wanted heard first. I chose the Motion for (a Default) Summary Judgment. The judge agreed that might be the best place to start. He pointed out that Asset Acceptance, LLC, had objected to my counterclaim; the Motion for Summary Judgment was based on Asset Acceptance, LLC's, not answering the counterclaim. The judge ruled that the counterclaim would have to be stricken as I had not asked leave of the court to file it. Therefore, my Motion for Summary Judgment based on Asset Acceptance, LLC's, not answering the counterclaim was moot. Air rushed out of my lungs.

"However," the judge quickly interjected, "I am giving the Defendant (me) leave of the court right now to file a counterclaim." Air rushed back into my lungs!!

Amanda Duffy said, "But, judge . . ."

The judge interrupted her and repeated rather firmly, "I am giving the Defendant leave of the court right now to file a counterclaim." Then looking at me he said, "And if you desire to file another Motion To Dismiss at any time in the future, the court will hear your motion immediately."

The judge then asked what was next. I answered I would like to have my Motion To Strike Card Agreement heard. The judge ruled in favor of me on the motion, but without prejudice. He looked at Amanda Duffy and said, "I give you 20 days to come up with the correct Card Agreement." I knew I could still poke holes in the correct Card Agreement.

"Next?" the judge asked, to which I answered, "Motion To Strike Bill of Sale and Assignment."

The judge again ruled in favor of me, but without prejudice. He gave Amanda Duffy 20 days to come up with "Exhibit 1" that should have been attached to the Complaint originally. I knew I could still poke holes also in that.

JDB's are in the business of quickly getting default judgments as 90% of the Defendants (consumers) never even answer the Summons and Complaint. Having to go back and correct errors and locating correct documentation is timely and costly to them. Many times JDBs will prefer to simply get out of the case altogether.

The judge put off ruling on the Motion To Strike the Affidavit as he said it was "evidentiary" and would need to be heard in trial. The judge then admonished Amanda Duffy for not being cooperative in communication with me. I admit I smiled inside.

I felt so empowered to realize I had gone from frightened, unknowledgeable, and powerless, to being in a courtroom before a judge across the table from one of the largest, oldest debt collection companies in the country, and it was going my way!

# IN THE COUNTY COURT IN AND FOR POLK COUNTY, FLORIDA
## CIVIL DIVISION

ASSET ACCEPTANCE, LLC

      Plaintiff,

vs.                        Case No. 5311CC1415

SHEILA R. MUNOZ,

      Defendant.

## COUNTERCLAIM AFTER DISCOVERY

COMES NOW the Defendant, SHEILA R. MUNOZ, pro se, pursuant to Fl.R.Civ.P. Rule 1.170, and states the following:

1.      Defendant, Sheila R. Munoz, pro se, is a natural person and a "consumer" as defined by FDCPA 15 U.S.C. (6) § 1692a: "any natural person obligated or allegedly obligated to pay any debt." Defendant resides in Lakeland, Polk County, Florida.

2.      Defendant is unschooled in law and asks the Court to take Judicial Notice of the enunciation of principles as stated in *Haines v. Kerner*, 404 U.S. 519, wherein the Court has directed that those who are unschooled in law making pleadings and/or complaints shall have the Court look to the substance of the pleadings rather than the form.

Fl.R.Civ.P. Rule 1.190: "At every stage of the action the court must disregard any error or defect in the proceedings which does not affect the substantial rights of the parties."

3.      Plaintiff, Asset Acceptance, LLC, is a corporation organized under the laws of Delaware (see "Bill of Sale and Assignment," Exhibit 1), engaged in the business of collecting debt in this and other states. Plaintiff is a "debt collector" as defined by 15 U.S.C. § 1692a(6): "A debt collector is any person who uses any instrumentality of interstate commerce or the mails in any business, the principal purpose of which is the collection of any debts, or who

regularly collect or attempts to collect, directly or indirectly, debts owed or due or asserted to be owed or due to another."

Asset Acceptance was founded in 1962 "for the purpose of purchasing and collecting charged off consumer receivables" (Asset Acceptance website). Therefore, it should be assumed Plaintiff would know the laws as it pertains to their industry.

4. On or about April 4, 2011, Plaintiff served the Defendant with a Complaint for "Breach of Contract" and "Stated Account."

5. Plaintiff violated Fl.R.Civ.P. Rule 1.130 on no less than three counts: "All bonds, notes, bills of exchange, contracts, accounts, or documents upon which action may be brought or defense made, or a copy thereof or a copy of the portions thereof material to the pleadings, shall be incorporated in or attached to the pleading."

A. Plaintiff failed to attach a copy of the written instrument (Contract), upon which the Complaint was based, to the Complaint.

B. Plaintiff, in the alleged "Bill of Sale and Assignment" (see Exhibit 1 attached) that was attached to Plaintiff's Complaint as a basis of the Complaint, referenced "Exhibit 1" as one of the bases of Plaintiff's Complaint. There was no "Exhibit 1" attached to Plaintiff's Complaint.

C. Although Plaintiff claims to have been delivered "the final electronic file" (see Exhibit 1 attached), Plaintiff has not attached those records and has attached an "Affidavit" (see Exhibit 7 attached) by Crystal Janus in lieu of a written instrument or any records pertaining to the account.

(1) On information and belief, the affiant, Crystal Janus, was never employed by the original creditor.

(2) On information and belief, the affiant, Crystal Janus, was never in a fiduciary or any other position to examine the original creditor's open books for the account of the alleged debt.

(3) On information and belief, the affiant, Crystal Janus, does not have personal knowledge of the original creditor's cre-

ation, maintenance, issuance, and tracking of the billing or statements as they pertain to the alleged debt.

(4) The notarization is faulty: there is no verification of the identity of the affiant.

(5) The Affidavit attached is no more than hearsay:

**FS 90.801 Hearsay; definitions; exceptions.—**

**(c) "Hearsay" is a statement, other than one made by the declarant while testifying at the trial or hearing, offered in evidence to prove the truth of the matter asserted.**

**(2) A statement is not hearsay if the declarant testifies at the trial or hearing and is subject to cross-examination concerning the statement and the statement is:"**

(6) In discovery, Plaintiff did not list Crystal Janus as a witness they were intending to have testify.

D.  In the case of *Sollami v. Eaton*, 2002 Ill. Lexis 331, Docket Nos. 91284, 91378, it states:

"The court also reviewed the requirement that the affidavit attach sworn or certified copies of records upon which the affiant relied. Plaintiff argued that this requirement was merely technical. But the court disagreed. ". . . [T]his requirement is in extricably linked to the provisions requiring specific factual support in the affidavit itself . . . We are unwilling to allow the simple production of an expert's conclusion 'to become a free pass to trial.'" In this case, striking Plaintiff's expert affidavit was upheld because of the failure to attach the pertinent records. Plaintiff thus had no expert affidavit."

E.  The notarization of the Affidavit is faulty: there is no verification of identification of the person Crystal Janus.

6.      On April 19, 2011, Defendant filed with the Clerk of Court, Defendant's Answer to Complaint and Summons, as well as mailed

by Certified Return Receipt the Answer to the Plaintiff's employee/attorney.

Defendant offered as an Affirmative Defense that the alleged debt is outside of the Statute of Limitations of three years, since Asset Acceptance is organized under Delaware Law as stated in the alleged "Bill of Sale and Assignment."

The Defendant offered many other Affirmative Defenses in the Answer, as well as in the document, "Additional Affirmative Defenses After Discovery."

7.      On May 6, 2011, the Plaintiff served on the Defendant First Set of Interrogatories, Request for Admissions, and Request for Production of Documents.

Defendant served Answers to these requests on the Plaintiff's employee/attorney June 10, 2011 (within 30 days + 5 for mail as required by Fl.R.Civ.P. Rules 1.340, 1.350, and 1.370), and Notices of Service were filed with the Court.

8.      On May 9, 2011, Defendant served Plaintiff's employee/attorney First Set of Interrogatories, Request for Admissions, and Request for Production of Documents.

Plaintiff violated Fl.R.Civ,P. Rules 1.340, 1.350, and 1.370. The Interrogatories, Request for Admissions, and Request for Production of Documents were partially answered by the Plaintiff and served on the Defendant June 23, 2011 (40 days + 5 for mail) (see "Notices of Service," Exhibit 2), no less than 10 days after the deadline on each one.

It should be assumed Plaintiff, as having been in the debt collection business since 1962, would know the law as it pertains to something as basic as deadlines for answering discovery.

9.      On May 10, 2011, Defendant filed with the Clerk of Court and mailed to the Plaintiff's employee/attorney a Sworn Denial, a Motion to Strike Affidavit, a Motion to Strike Card Agreement, and a Motion to Strike Affidavit.

The Plaintiff has not objected to any of these, nor has Plaintiff returned Defendant's call to set a date for a hearing on the Motions. A letter was subsequently mailed to the Court requesting the Honorable Judge to set a date for a hearing on the Motions.

10.     On June 25, 2011, in the Plaintiff's answer to Request to Produce Documents was a copy of the alleged "Notification Letter" from Plaintiff that notified the Defendant that Plaintiff had purchased the alleged debt and was the new owner of the debt.

The Plaintiff violated F.S. § 559.715. The Bill of Sale and Assignment (Exhibit 1 attached) shows the debt was allegedly purchased June 29, 2010. The copy of the Letter of Notification (Exhibit 3 attached) which the Plaintiff provided during discovery is dated August 9, 2010, 42 days after the alleged purchase, no less than 12 days after the deadline.

It should be assumed Plaintiff would know the law as it pertains to something as basic as meeting deadlines for sending a Notification Letter in regards to purchasing a debt. This is the fourth deadline Plaintiff has missed.

Plaintiff's pattern of ignoring timeframes as stipulated by law portrays Plaintiff's blatant disregard to the law as it pertains to Plaintiff's industry, in which Plaintiff has done business since 1962.

11.     Plaintiff alleges in the alleged "Bill of Sale and Assignment" that Citibank delivered "for value" "the Accounts listed in Exhibit 1 and final electronic file" (see Exhibit 1 attached).

    A.  Defendant translates the meaning of delivered "'for value' and 'the Accounts listed in Exhibit 1 and final electronic file'" to mean "the Plaintiff purchased any and all the pertinent records to prove Plaintiff's allegations on the alleged debt and has such alleged evidence in Plaintiff's possession."

        (1) On June 23, 2011, Plaintiff served on Defendant a "Notice of Production From Non-Party" that, outside of any objections from any party, a Subpoena Duces Tecum (Exhibit 4 attached) would be served on Citicorp Credit Services, Inc., USA, commanding to produce the card member agreement; checks; itemized state-

ments reflecting purchases, payments, and financial charges; and signed application.

(2) During discovery, Plaintiff admits (Exhibit 5 attached) Plaintiff does not have these records/documents in their possession.

(3) Plaintiff violated 15 U.S.C. § 1692e(2)(A) as it relates to "final electronic file": "A debt collector may not use any false, deceptive, or misleading representation or means in connection with the collection of any debt."

The fact that Plaintiff alleges in the "Bill of Sale and Assignment" (Exhibit 1) that Citibank delivered to Plaintiff "final electronic file" and then subpoenaing Citicorp Credit Services, Inc., for the same documentation is, at the least, deceptive.

B.  Plaintiff violated 15 U.S.C. § 1692e(2)(A) as it relates the Card Agreement attached to the Plaintiff's Complaint: "A debt collector may not use any false, deceptive, or misleading representation or means in connection with the collection of any debt."

In the Subpoena Duces Tecum, Plaintiff commands the Card Agreement be produced by Citicorp Credit Services, Inc., although Plaintiff attached an alleged Card Agreement to Plaintiff's Complaint, upon which Plaintiff based the Complaint.

The Card Agreement (Exhibit 6 attached) that was attached to Plaintiff's Complaint displays a date of 2006 rather than 2004, the date Plaintiff alleges the alleged debt was initiated. Defendant filed a Motion To Strike the Card Agreement.

12.     As a result of the acts by the Plaintiff listed above, the Defendant has suffered personal stress symptoms of nausea, headaches, nervousness, embarrassment, sleeplessness, severe irritability, and marital stress, causing increased medical expenses, paper and printing expenses, postage, travel expenses to and from Clerk of Court, hours of time away from family, and loss of income. This has transferred to Defendant's terminally ill daughter under Defendant's care and may possibly have shortened Defendant's daughter's life even further, causing emotional stress on the Defendant.

Furthermore, working against this Complaint has cost Defendant precious hours away from Defendant's terminally ill daughter, precious time which can never be retrieved.

## FIRST CLAIM FOR RELIEF

13. Defendant repeats and re-alleges and incorporates by reference paragraphs 1 through 12.

A. "The FDCPA is a strict liability statute, and one violation is sufficient to establish liability." *Bentley v. Great Lakes Coll. Bureau*, 6 F.3d 60 (2d Cir. 1993).

B. The FDCPA was passed to eliminate abusive debt collection practices by debt collectors, to insure that those debt collectors who refrain from using abusive debt collection practices are not competitively disadvantaged, and to promote consistent State action to protect consumers against debt collection abuses. 15 U.S.C. § 1692.

C. The Plaintiff violated 15 U.S.C. § 1692e(2)(A) by misrepresenting the character, amount, or legal status of any debt, by attempting to collect on an alleged debt when it was known by the Plaintiff that the Complaint filed was not precluded by a 30-day notice of the alleged Sale and Assignment of the debt.

D. The Plaintiff violated 15 U.S.C. § 1692e(2)(A) by misrepresenting themselves as having in Plaintiff's possession the "final electronic file," upon which Plaintiff's Complaint was based.

E. The Plaintiff violated 15 U.S.C. § 1692e(5) by filing an action on an alleged debt that is outside the Statute of Limitations by Delaware law.

F. Factors considered by Court, including, but not limited to, meeting deadlines stipulated by law:

15 U.S.C. § 1692k "In determining the amount of liability in any action under subsection (a) of this section, the courts shall consider, among other relevant factors –

(1) "in any individual action under subsection (a)(2)(A) of this section, the frequency and persistence of noncompliance by the debt collector, the nature of such noncompliance, and the extent to which such noncompliance was intentional;"

G.  15 U.S.C. § 1692k: "Any debt collector who fails to comply with any provision of this title with respect to any person is liable to such person in an amount equal to the sum of—

(1) any actual damage sustained by such person as a result of such failure;

(2) (A) in the case of any action by an individual, such additional damages as the court may allow, but not exceeding $1,000;

(3) in the case of any successful action to enforce the foregoing liability, the costs of the action, together with a reasonable attorney's fee as determined by the court. On a finding by the court that an action under this section was brought in bad faith and for the purpose of harassment, the court may award to the defendant attorney's fees reasonable in relation to the work expended and costs.

14.     As a result of the above violations of the FDCPA, the Plaintiff is liable to the Defendant for declaratory judgment, actual damages, statutory damages, and attorney fees and costs.

## SECOND CLAIM FOR RELIEF

15.     Plaintiff repeats and re-alleges and incorporates by reference paragraphs 1-14.

16.     The Plaintiff violated the Florida Rules of Civil Procedure, including, but not limited to, the following:

A.  The Plaintiff violated Fl.R.Civ.P. Rule 1.130 on no less than 3 counts, Attaching Copy of Cause of Action and Exhibits: "(a) Instruments Attached. All bonds, notes, bills of exchange, contracts, accounts, or documents upon which action may be brought or defense made, or a copy thereof or a copy of the portions thereof material to the pleadings, shall be incorporated in or attached to the pleading. No papers shall be unnecessarily annexed as exhibits. The pleadings shall contain no unnecessary recitals of deeds, documents, contracts, or other instruments."

(1) Plaintiff did not attach the alleged Contract upon which "Breach of Contract" was based.

(2) Plaintiff did not attach the correct alleged Card Agreement upon which Plaintiff's Complaint was based, but rather is issuing a Subpoena Duces Tecum for it from Citicorp Credit Services, Inc.

(3) Plaintiff did not attach "Exhibit 1" specifying the account on which Plaintiff's Complaint was based and referenced in the alleged "Bill of Sale and Assignment."

17.     As a result of the above violations of the Florida Rules of Civil Procedure, the Plaintiff is liable to the Defendant for declaratory judgment, actual damages, statutory damages, and attorney fees and costs.

### THIRD CLAIM FOR RELIEF

18.     Plaintiff repeats and re-alleges and incorporates by reference paragraphs 1-17.

19.     The Plaintiff violated the Florida Statutes Title 33, PART VI. CONSUMER COLLECTION PRACTICES, including, but not limited to, the following:

(1) The Plaintiff violated FS § 559.715. Plaintiff failed to give Defendant written notice of assignment within 30 days.

(2) The Plaintiff violated FS § 559.72(9) on no less than 3 counts: In collecting consumer debts, no person shall "Claim, attempt, or threaten to enforce a debt when such persons know that the debt is not legitimate or assert the existence of some other legal right when such person knows that the right does not exist."

Plaintiff filed an action on alleged debt on which they should have known they could not file,

    A.  Since their compliance with FS 559.715 did not preclude the lawsuit;

    B.  Since the alleged debt was outside the Statute of Limitations by Delaware law; and

    C.  Since they did not have in their possession nor did they attach the copies of the documents upon which Plaintiff based the Complaints.

20.    Plaintiff's acts, as described above, were done intentionally with the purpose of coercing the Defendant to pay an alleged debt.

21.    As a result of the above violations of the Florida Statutes Title 33, PART VI. CONSUMER COLLECTION PRACTICES, the Plaintiff is liable to the Defendant for declaratory judgment, actual damages, statutory damages, and attorney fees and costs.

WHEREFORE, Defendant respectfully prays that judgment be entered against the Plaintiff for the following:

A.    Declaratory judgment that Plaintiff's conduct violated the FDCPA, and declaratory and injunctive relief for the Plaintiff's violation of the Florida Consumer Collection Practice Act;

B.    Actual and Statutory damages pursuant to 15 USC § 1692k;

C.    Actual and Statutory damages pursuant to FCCPA § 559.72;

D.    Costs and reasonable attorney's fees pursuant to 15 USC § 2692k, FS 559.72, and inherent powers, and/or;

E.    For such other and further relief as may be just and proper.

Dated the 29th of June, 2011.

_____

███████████████████

SHEILA R. MUNOZ, Defendant

## CERTIFICATE OF SERVICE

I hereby certify that a copy hereof has been furnished by First Class Mail to Plaintiff's employee/attorney this 29th day of June 2011, to the following address:

Amanda R. Duffy
Asset Acceptance, LLC
PO Box 9065
Brandon, FL 33509

_____

SHEILA R. MUNOZ, Defendant

# IN THE COUNTY COURT IN AND FOR POLK COUNTY, FLORIDA
## CIVIL DIVISION

ASSET ACCEPTANCE, LLC

       Plaintiff,

vs.                  Case No. 5311CC1415

SHEILA R. MUNOZ,

       Defendant.

## MOTION TO DISMISS

COMES NOW the Defendant, SHEILA R. MUNOZ, pro se, pursuant to Fl.R.Civ.P. Rule 1.160, and states the following: Defendant hereby moves the Court to dismiss Plaintiff's Complaint with prejudice. The bases for this Motion are set forth in the accompanying Memorandum.

Dated the 29th of June, 2011

███████████████████████████
_____

             SHEILA R. MUNOZ, Defendant

## CERTIFICATE OF SERVICE

I hereby certify that a copy hereof has been furnished by First Class Mail to Plaintiff's employee/attorney this 29th day of June 2011, to the following address:

Amanda R. Duffy
Asset Acceptance, LLC
PO Box 9065
Brandon, FL 33509

███████████████████████████
_____

             SHEILA R. MUNOZ, Defendant

IN THE COUNTY COURT IN AND FOR POLK COUNTY, FLORIDA
CIVIL DIVISION

ASSET ACCEPTANCE, LLC

        Plaintiff,

vs.                      Case No. 5311CC1415

SHEILA R. MUNOZ,

        Defendant.

## MEMORANDUM IN SUPPORT OF MOTION TO DISMISS

### FACTS

1.      Defendant Sheila R. Munoz, pro se, is a natural person and resides in Lakeland, Polk County, Florida.

2.      Defendant is unschooled in law.

3.      Plaintiff, Asset Acceptance, LLC, is a corporation organized under the laws of Delaware (see "Bill of Sale and Assignment," Exhibit 1), engaged in the business of collecting debt in this and other states.

Asset Acceptance was founded in 1962 "for the purpose of purchasing and collecting charged off consumer receivables" (Asset Acceptance website).

4.      On or about April 4, 2011, Plaintiff served the Defendant with a Complaint for "Breach of Contract" and "Stated Account."

5.      Plaintiff failed to attach a copy of the written instrument (Contract), upon which the Complaint was based, to the Complaint.

6.      Plaintiff, in the alleged "Bill of Sale and Assignment" (see Exhibit 1 attached) that was attached to Plaintiff's Complaint as a basis of the Complaint, referenced "Exhibit 1" as one of the bases of Plaintiff's Complaint. There was no "Exhibit 1" attached to Plaintiff's Complaint.

7.     Although Plaintiff claims to have been delivered "the final electronic file" (see Exhibit 1 attached), Plaintiff has not attached those records and has attached an "Affidavit" (see Exhibit 7 attached) by Crystal Janus in lieu of a written instrument or any records pertaining to the account.

In discovery, Plaintiff did not list Crystal Janus as a witness they were intending to have testify.

8.     On April 19, 2011, Defendant filed with the Clerk of Court, Defendant's Answer to Complaint and Summons, as well as mailed by Certified Return Receipt the Answer to the Plaintiff's employee/ attorney.

Defendant has denied the alleged debt and offered Affirmative Defenses in the Answer, as well as in the document, "Additional Affirmative Defenses After Discovery."

9.     The Statute of Limitations for open accounts in the state of Delaware is three years. Asset Acceptance was organized under Delaware law as stated in the alleged "Bill of Sale and Assignment" attached to Plaintiff's Complaint.

10.     On May 6, 2011, the Plaintiff served on the Defendant First Set of Interrogatories, Request for Admissions, and Request for Production of Documents.

11.     Defendant served Answers to these requests on the Plaintiff's employee/attorney June 10, 2011 (within 30 days + 5 for mail), and Notices of Service were filed with the Court.

12.     On May 9, 2011, Defendant served Plaintiff's employee/attorney First Set of Interrogatories, Request for Admissions, and Request for Production of Documents.

These were partially answered by the Plaintiff and served on the Defendant June 23, 2011 (40 days + 5 for mail) (see "Notices of Service," Exhibit 2), at least 10 days late.

13.     On May 10, 2011, Defendant filed with the Clerk of Court and mailed to the Plaintiff's employee/attorney a Sworn Denial, a Mo-

tion to Strike Affidavit, a Motion to Strike Card Agreement, and a Motion to Strike Affidavit.

The Plaintiff has not objected to any of these, nor has Plaintiff returned Defendant's call to set a date for a hearing on the Motions.

A letter was subsequently mailed to the Court requesting the Honorable Judge to set a date for a hearing on the Motions.

14.  On June 25, 2011, in the Plaintiff's answer to Request to Produce Documents was a copy of the alleged "Notification Letter" from Plaintiff that notified the Defendant that Plaintiff had purchased the alleged debt and was the new owner of the debt.

The Bill of Sale and Assignment (Exhibit 1 attached) shows the debt was allegedly purchased June 29, 2010. The copy of the Letter of Notification (Exhibit 3 attached) which the Plaintiff provided during discovery is dated August 9, 2010, 42 days after the alleged purchase, no less than 12 days late.

15.  Plaintiff alleges in the alleged "Bill of Sale and Assignment" that Citibank delivered "for value" "the Accounts listed in Exhibit 1 and final electronic file" (see Exhibit 1 attached).

16.  In the Subpoena Duces Tecum (Exhibit 4 attached), Plaintiff commands that the Card Agreement be produced by Citicorp Credit Services, Inc., although Plaintiff attached an alleged Card Agreement to Plaintiff's Complaint, upon which Plaintiff based the Complaint.

The date of 2006 is on the Card Agreement (Exhibit 6 attached) that was attached to the Complaint, rather than 2004, the date Plaintiff alleges the alleged debt was initiated. Defendant filed a Motion To Strike the Card Agreement.

### ARGUMENTS

1.  Defendant is a "consumer" as defined by FDCPA 15 U.S.C. (6) § 1692a: "any natural person obligated or allegedly obligated to pay any debt."

2.      As stated in *Haines v. Kerner*, 404 U.S. 519, the Court is directed that those who are unschooled in law making pleadings and/or complaints shall have the Court look to the substance of the pleadings rather than the form.

Fl.R.Civ.P. Rule 1.190: "At every stage of the action the court must disregard any error or defect in the proceedings which does not affect the substantial rights of the parties."

3.      Plaintiff is a "debt collector" as defined by 15 U.S.C. § 1692a(6): "A debt collector is any person who uses any instrumentality of interstate commerce or the mails in any business, the principal purpose of which is the collection of any debts, or who regularly collect or attempts to collect, directly or indirectly, debts owed or due or asserted to be owed or due to another."

4.      It should be assumed Plaintiff would know the laws as it pertains to their industry since they have been in business since 1962 in the debt collecting business.

5.      Plaintiff violated Fl.R.Civ.P. Rule 1.130 on three counts: "All bonds, notes, bills of exchange, contracts, accounts, or documents upon which action may be brought or defense made, or a copy thereof or a copy of the portions thereof material to the pleadings, shall be incorporated in or attached to the pleading."

        A. Plaintiff did not attach the alleged Contract upon which Plaintiff's "Breach of Contract" Complaint was based.

        B. Plaintiff did not attach "Exhibit 1" referenced as being "the Accounts listed" in the alleged "Bill of Sale and Assignment," upon which Plaintiff's Complaint was based.

        C. Plaintiff did not attach the correct alleged Card Agreement upon which Plaintiff's Complaint was based, but instead is now subpoenaing the Agreement from Citicorp Credit Services, Inc.

6.      In regard to the alleged "Affidavit" (see Exhibit 7 attached) attached to Plaintiff's Complaint:

A.  On information and belief, the affiant, Crystal Janus, was never an employee of the alleged original creditor.

B.  On information and belief, the affiant, Crystal Janus, was never in a fiduciary or any other position to examine the original creditor's open books for the account of the alleged debt.

C.  On information and belief, the affiant, Crystal Janus, does not have personal knowledge of the original creditor's creation, maintenance, issuance, and tracking of the billing or statements as they pertain to the alleged debt.

D.  The notarization is faulty: there is no verification of the identity of the affiant.

E.  The Affidavit attached to Plaintiff's Complaint is no more than hearsay:

FS 90.801 Hearsay; definitions; exceptions.—

(1) The following definitions apply under this chapter:

(c) "Hearsay" is a statement, other than one made by the declarant while testifying at the trial or hearing, offered in evidence to prove the truth of the matter asserted.

(2) A statement is not hearsay if the declarant testifies at the trial or hearing and is subject to cross-examination concerning the statement and the statement is:"

F.  In the case of *Sollami v. Eaton*, 2002 Ill. Lexis 331, Docket Nos. 91284, 91378, it states:

"The court also reviewed the requirement that the affidavit attach sworn or certified copies of records upon which the affiant relied. Plaintiff argued that this requirement was merely technical. But the court disagreed. ". . . [T]his requirement is in extricably linked to the provisions requiring specific factual support in the affidavit itself . . . We are unwilling to allow the simple production of an expert's conclusion 'to become a free pass to trial.'" In this case, striking Plaintiff's expert affidavit was upheld because of the failure to attach the pertinent records. Plaintiff thus had no expert affidavit."

7.      Plaintiff violated Fl.R.Civ.P. Rule 1.350 by serving Plaintiff's answers to Request for Documents at least 10 days after the deadline. It should be assumed Plaintiff, as having been in the debt collection business since 1962, would know the law as it pertains to something as basic as deadlines for answering discovery.

8.      Plaintiff violated Fl.R.Civ.P. Rule 1.370 by serving Plaintiff's answers to Request for Admissions at least 10 days after the deadline. It should be assumed Plaintiff, as having been in the debt collection business since 1962, would know the law as it pertains to something as basic as deadlines for answering discovery.

9.      Plaintiff violated Fl.R.Civ.P. Rule 1.340 by serving Plaintiff's answers to Interrogatories at least 10 days after the deadline. It should be assumed Plaintiff, as having been in the debt collection business since 1962, would know the law as it pertains to something as basic as deadlines for answering discovery.

10.      Plaintiff violated FS 559.715 in that Plaintiff failed to meet the deadline in supplying the Defendant with a Notification of Assignment Letter by 12 days

11.      Plaintiff failed to meet deadlines on no less than four different occasions. Plaintiff has been in the business of debt collecting since 1962. It should be assumed they know the law as it pertains to deadlines and their industry. Plaintiff's habitually serving documents late portrays a blatant disregard for the law as it pertains to their industry.

12.      Plaintiff violated 15 U.S.C. § 1692e on no less than two occasions: "A debt collector may not use any false, deceptive, or misleading representation or means in connection with the collection of any debt":

A.  In the alleged "Bill of Sale and Assignment" (Exhibit 1 attached) Defendant translates the meaning of delivered "'for value' and 'the Accounts listed in Exhibit 1 and final electronic file'" to mean "the Plaintiff purchased any and all the pertinent records to prove Plaintiff's allegations on the alleged debt and has such alleged evidence in Plaintiff's possession."

However, on June 23, 2011, Plaintiff served on Defendant a "Notice of Production From Non-Party" that, outside of any objections from any party, a Subpoena Duces Tecum (Exhibit 4 attached) would be served on Citicorp Credit Services, Inc., USA, commanding to produce the card member agreement; checks; itemized statements reflecting purchases, payments, and financial charges; and signed application.

Additionally, during discovery, Plaintiff admits (Exhibit 5 attached) Plaintiff does not have these records/documents in their possession.

The fact that Plaintiff alleges in the "Bill of Sale and Assignment" (Exhibit 1 attached) that Citibank delivered to Plaintiff "final electronic file" is, at the least, deceptive to the Defendant by virtue of the verbiage used and violates 15 U.S.C. § 1692e(2)(A).

      B. Plaintiff did not attach the correct alleged Card Agreement (Exhibit 6 attached) upon which Plaintiff's Complaint was based, but instead is now subpoenaing the Agreement from Citicorp Credit Services, Inc. By attaching to the Complaint the wrong alleged Card Agreement, Plaintiff violated 15 U.S.C. ss 1692e(2)(A).

13.    The Plaintiff violated 15 U.S.C. § 1692e(2)(A) on no less than 2 counts:

      A. By misrepresenting the character, amount, or legal status of any debt, by attempting to collect on an alleged debt when it was known by the Plaintiff that the Complaint filed was not precluded by a 30-day notice of the alleged Sale and Assignment of the debt.

      B. By misrepresenting themselves as having in Plaintiff's possession the "final electronic file," upon which Plaintiff's Complaint was based.

14.    The Plaintiff violated 15 U.S.C. 0167 1692e(5) by filing an action on an alleged debt that is outside the Statute of Limitations by Delaware law.

15.    The Plaintiff violated FS § 559.72(9) on no less than 3 counts:

In collecting consumer debts, no person shall "Claim, attempt, or threaten to enforce a debt when such persons know that the debt is not legitimate or assert the existence of some other legal right when such person knows that the right does not exist."

A.  Plaintiff filed an action on an alleged debt on which they should have known they could not file since they did not have the copies of the contracts, accounts, or documents upon which Plaintiff based the Complaints.

B.  Plaintiff filed an action on an alleged debt on which they should have known they could not file, since their compliance with FS § 559.715 did not preclude the lawsuit.

C.  Plaintiff filed an action on an alleged debt that was outside the Statute of Limitations by Delaware law.

## CONCLUSION

WHEREFORE, for the reasons stated above, Defendant prays the Court will grant this Motion to Dismiss with prejudice.

Dated this 29th day of June, 2011,

_____

SHEILA R. MUNOZ, Defendant

# CERTIFICATE OF SERVICE

I hereby certify that a copy hereof has been furnished by First Class Mail to Plaintiff's employee/attorney this 29th day of June 2011, to the following address:

Amanda R. Duffy
Asset Acceptance, LLC
PO Box 9065
Brandon, FL 33509

SHEILA R. MUNOZ, Defendant

June 30, 2011

Amanda R Duffy
Asset Acceptance, LLC
PO Box 9065
Bartow, FL 33509

Dear Ms. Duffy:

I have filed with the Court 4 Motions: Motion To Strike Affidavit, Motion To Strike Card Agreement, Motion To Strike Bill of Sale and Assignment, and Motion To Dismiss.

These Motions need to be set for Hearing. As you know, a trial cannot be set while there are pending Motions.

I have attempted to contact you via phone in this regard, but have not received a response to any voicemail, although your greeting indicates you will return the call. Please contact me via mail at the above address as to several dates that would work for you for a Hearing on these matters. I will be happy, then, to contact the Court and get a Hearing(s) scheduled.

I look forward to your response.

Sincerely,

Sheila R. Munoz

Cc:     The Honorable
        PO Box
        Drawer
        Bartow, FL 33831-9000

IN THE COUNTY COURT IN AND FOR POLK COUNTY, FLORIDA
CIVIL DIVISION

ASSET ACCEPTANCE, LLC

        Plaintiff,

vs.                          Case No. 5311CC1415

SHEILA R. MUNOZ,

        Defendant.

## MOTION TO COMPEL

COMES NOW the Defendant, SHEILA R. MUNOZ, pro se, pursuant to Fl.R.Civ.P. Rule 1.160, and states the following: Defendant hereby moves the Court to compel Plaintiff to set Hearings for the four (4) Motions filed with the Court: Motion To Dismiss, Motion To Strike Card Agreement, Motion To Strike Affidavit, and Motion To Strike Card Agreement, based on the following facts:

1.     The Defendant filed with the Court a Motion To Strike Card Agreement, a Motion To Strike Affidavit, and a Motion To Strike Bill of Sale and Assignment on May 9, 2011. To date, no Response from the Plaintiff has been received nor has a Hearing been set.

2.     The Defendant filed with the Court a Motion To Dismiss June 29, 2011. To date, no Response from the Plaintiff has been received nor has a Hearing been set.

3.     A good faith effort has been made to set dates for Hearing(s) on the four Motions. On June 22, 2011, a phone message was left with Plaintiff's attorney asking for setting of Hearing(s) on the Motions. No return call was received. On June 29, 2011, a letter was mailed to the Plaintiff's attorney/employee asking for setting of Hearing(s), with a copy to the Court. No response has been received.

4.     The Plaintiff has refused to respond or to set Hearing(s) on the four Motions. Since the Plaintiff has refused to respond in a

timely manner, the Defendant moves the honorable Court to compel the Plaintiff to set Hearing(s) WITHIN FIVE DAYS on the four Motions filed with the Court.

Dated the 20th of July, 2011

_____
SHEILA R. MUNOZ, Defendant

## CERTIFICATE OF SERVICE

I hereby certify that a copy hereof has been furnished by fax and First Class Mail to Plaintiff's employee/attorney this 20th day of July 2011, to the following address:

Amanda R. Duffy
Asset Acceptance, LLC
PO Box 9065
Brandon, FL 33509
Fax: 813.983.2519

_____
SHEILA R. MUNOZ, Defendant

IN THE COUNTY COURT IN AND FOR POLK COUNTY, FLORIDA
CIVIL DIVISION

ASSET ACCEPTANCE, LLC

        Plaintiff,

vs.                     Case No. 5311CC1415

SHEILA R. MUNOZ,

        Defendant.

## MOTION FOR SUMMARY JUDGMENT WITH PREJUDICE

        COMES NOW the Defendant, SHEILA R. MUNOZ, pro se, pursuant to Fed.R.Civ.Pro. 56*[1], who respectfully moves this honorable Court to grant a default Summary Judgment with prejudice against Plaintiff and to demand declaratory judgment and relief in statutory, actual, and punitive damages as allowed by law and as outlined in the attached Memorandum.

Plaintiff has failed to answer the Counterclaim filed with the Court June 29, 2011 within 20 days.

By default, there is no genuine issue as to any material fact. Defendant is entitled to a default judgment as a matter of law. The bases for this Motion are set forth in the accompanying Memorandum.

Dated the 26th day of July, 2011

                                ████████████

                                SHEILA R. MUNOZ, Defendant

# CERTIFICATE OF SERVICE

I hereby certify that a copy hereof has been furnished by First Class Mail to Plaintiff's employee/attorney this 26th day of July 2011, to the following address:

Amanda R. Duffy
Asset Acceptance, LLC
PO Box 9065
Brandon, FL 33509

SHEILA R. MUNOZ, Defendant

# IN THE COUNTY COURT IN AND FOR POLK COUNTY, FLORIDA
## CIVIL DIVISION

ASSET ACCEPTANCE, LLC

      Plaintiff,

vs.                         Case No. 5311CC1415

SHEILA R. MUNOZ,

      Defendant.

## MEMORANDUM IN SUPPORT OF
## MOTION FOR SUMMARY JUDGMENT

## FACTS

1.      Defendant, Sheila R. Munoz, pro se, is a natural person and a "consumer" as defined by FDCPA 15 U.S.C. (6) § 1692a: "any natural person obligated or allegedly obligated to pay any debt." Defendant resides in Lakeland, Polk County, Florida.

2.      Defendant is unschooled in law and asks the Court to take Judicial Notice of the enunciation of principles as stated in *Haines v. Kerner*, 404 U.S. 519, wherein the Court has directed that those who are unschooled in law making pleadings and/or complaints shall have the Court look to the substance of the pleadings rather than the form.

Fl.R.Civ.P. Rule 1.190: "At every stage of the action the court must disregard any error or defect in the proceedings which does not affect the substantial rights of the parties."

3.      Plaintiff, Asset Acceptance, LLC, is a corporation organized under the laws of Delaware (see "Bill of Sale and Assignment," Exhibit 1 attached), engaged in the business of collecting debt in this and other states.

4.      Plaintiff is a "debt collector" as defined by 15 U.S.C. § 1692a(6): "A debt collector is any person who uses any instrumentality of interstate commerce or the mails in any business, the

principal purpose of which is the collection of any debts, or who regularly collect or attempts to collect, directly or indirectly, debts owed or due or asserted to be owed or due to another."

Asset Acceptance was founded in 1962 "for the purpose of purchasing and collecting charged off consumer receivables" (Asset Acceptance website). Therefore, it should be assumed Plaintiff would know the laws as it pertains to their industry.

5.      The Statute of Limitations under Delaware law is three years.

     A.  The Plaintiff alleges in their Complaint that the last payment on the alleged date was made on or about 4/30/2007.

     B.  The Statute of Limitations ended on or about 4/30/2010.

     C.  This alleged debt is time-barred.

6.      Defendant is judgment-execution proof, which was revealed to Plaintiff during discovery.

     A.  Defendant is Head of Household, having a terminally ill, totally and permanently disabled daughter who resides with the Defendant.

     B.  Defendant provides more than 50% of her terminally ill daughter's support.

     C.  Defendant's husband is also permanently and totally disabled, receiving SSDI.

     D.  Defendant resides in her homesteaded home that has negative equity.

     E.  Defendant self-employed with no garnishable wages.

     F.  Defendant has no other assets to which a judgment could be attached.

7.      On or about June 29, 2010, the Plaintiff was sold and assigned an alleged debt for collections by Citibank.

A.  The Bill of Sale and Assignment (see Exhibit 1 attached) does not indicate what consumer's account was sold and assigned.

B.  On August 9, 2010, Plaintiff supposedly sent to the Defendant a First Notice of the Sale and Assignment of the alleged debt to them by Citibank (see Exhibit 3 attached).

C.  ASSET ACCEPTANCE, LLC, sent the letter 42 days after the sale and assignment of the alleged debt, a violation of F.S. § 559.715, which requires such notice be sent within 30 days of the sale and assignment: "Assignment of consumer debts.--. . . the assignee must give the debtor written notice of such assignment within 30 days after the assignment."

D.  Defendant never received said letter.

E.  A copy of this letter was provided to the Defendant by the Plaintiff on June 25, 2011, in answer to Request For Production of Documents.

F.  FCCPA 559.715: "Assignment of consumer debts.--This part does not prohibit the assignment, by a creditor, of the right to bill and collect a consumer debt.

However, the assignee must give the debtor written notice of such assignment within 30 days after the assignment."

8.      On or about April 4, 2011, Plaintiff served the Defendant with a Complaint for "Breach of Contract" and "Stated Account."

A.  Plaintiff violated Fl.R.Civ.P. Rule 1.130 on no less than three counts: "All bonds, notes, bills of exchange, contracts, accounts, or documents upon which action may be brought or defense made, or a copy thereof or a copy of the portions thereof material to the pleadings, shall be incorporated in or attached to the pleading." (emphasis added)

(1) Plaintiff failed to attach to the Complaint a copy of the written instrument (Contract), upon which the Breach of Contract Complaint was based.

(2) Plaintiff, in the alleged "Bill of Sale and Assignment" (see Exhibit 1 attached) that was attached to Plaintiff's Complaint as a basis of the Complaint, referenced "Exhibit 1" as one of the bases of Plaintiff's Complaint. There was no "Exhibit 1" attached to Plaintiff's Complaint.

(3) Although Plaintiff claims to have received "the final electronic file" (see Exhibit 1 attached), Plaintiff has not attached those records and has attached an "Affidavit" (see Exhibit 7 attached) by Crystal Janus in lieu of a written instrument or any records pertaining to the account.

(a) On information and belief, the affiant, Crystal Janus, was never employed by the original creditor.

(b) On information and belief, the affiant, Crystal Janus, was never in a fiduciary or any other position to examine the original creditor's open books for the account of the alleged debt.

(c) On information and belief, the affiant, Crystal Janus, does not have personal knowledge of the original creditor's creation, maintenance, issuance, and tracking of the billing or statements as they pertain to the alleged debt.

(d) The notarization of Crystal Janus' signature is faulty: there is no verification of the identity of the affiant.

From Subsection 117.05(5) of the Florida Statutes: A notary public may not notarize a signature on a document unless he or she personally knows, or has satisfactory evidence, that the person whose signature is to be notarized is the individual who is described in and who is executing the instrument. A notary public shall certify in the certificate of acknowledgment or jurat the type of identification, either based on personal knowledge or other form of identification, upon which the notary public is relying. (emphasis added)

(e) The Affidavit Plaintiff attached to the Complaint is no more than hearsay:

**FS 90.801 Hearsay; definitions; exceptions.—**

**(c)** "Hearsay" is a statement, other than one made by the declarant while testifying at the trial or hearing, offered in evidence to prove the truth of the matter asserted.

**(b)** A statement is not hearsay if the declarant testifies at the trial or hearing and is subject to cross-examination concerning the statement . . .".

(f) In discovery, Plaintiff did not list Crystal Janus as a witness they were intending to have testify.

(g) In the case of Sollami v. Eaton, 2002 Ill. Lexis 331, Docket Nos. 91284, 91378, it states:

"The court also reviewed the requirement that the affidavit attach sworn or certified copies of records upon which the affiant relied. Plaintiff argued that this requirement was merely technical. But the court disagreed. ". . . [T]his requirement is in extricably linked to the provisions requiring specific factual support in the affidavit itself . . . We are unwilling to allow the simple production of an expert's conclusion 'to become a free pass to trial.'" In this case, striking Plaintiff's expert affidavit was upheld because of the failure to attach the pertinent records. Plaintiff thus had no expert affidavit."

9.     On April 19, 2011 (within 20 days as stipulated by law), Defendant filed with the Clerk of Court, Defendant's Answer to Complaint and Summons, as well as mailed by Certified Return Receipt the Answer to the Plaintiff's employee/attorney.

10.     On May 6, 2011, the Plaintiff served on the Defendant First Set of Interrogatories, Request for Admissions, and Request for Production of Documents.

Defendant served Answers to these requests on the Plaintiff's employee/attorney June 10, 2011 (within 30 days + 5 for mail as required by Fl.R.Civ.P. Rules 1.340, 1.350, and 1.370), and Notices of Service were filed with the Court.

11.     On May 9, 2011, Defendant served Plaintiff's employee/attorney First Set of Interrogatories, Request for Admissions, and Request for Production of Documents.

Plaintiff violated Fl.R.Civ,P. Rules 1.340, 1.350, and 1.370. The Interrogatories, Request for Admissions, and Request for Production of Documents were partially answered by the Plaintiff and served on the Defendant June 23, 2011 (40 days + 5 for mail) (see "Notices of Service," Exhibit 2), no less than 10 days after the deadline on each one (3 counts).

It should be assumed Plaintiff, as having been in the debt collection business since 1962, would know the law as it pertains to something as basic as deadlines for answering discovery.

Plaintiff's pattern of ignoring timeframes as stipulated by law portrays Plaintiff's blatant disregard to the law as it pertains to Plaintiff's industry, in which Plaintiff has done business since 1962.

Plaintiff ignored timeframes repeatedly, unnecessarily drawing out this sham pleading.

12.     On May 10, 2011, Defendant filed with the Clerk of Court and mailed to the Plaintiff's employee/attorney a Sworn Denial, a Motion to Strike Affidavit, a Motion to Strike Card Agreement, and a Motion to Strike Bill of Sale and Assignment.

    A.  The Plaintiff has not objected to any of these.

    B.  Five weeks later on June 22, 2011, upon instruction from Judge's office, Defendant called Plaintiff to request she set a hearing(s) on the 4 motions filed.

        (1) Another representative answered and transferred Defendant to Plaintiff's voicemail.

        (2) Plaintiff's voicemail greeting identified it was her voicemail and that she would return the call.

(3) Defendant left a request for her to set a hearing(s) on the 4 motions filed, asked her to call Defendant back, and left the number, repeating it at the end.

(4) Plaintiff did not respond.

C. On June 29, 2011, Defendant sent a letter to Plaintiff, (see Exhibit 8 attached), again requesting she set a hearing(s) on the 4 motions filed.

(1) Plaintiff did not respond to the letter nor set a hearing(s) for the 4 motions filed.

13.    Plaintiff alleges in the alleged "Bill of Sale and Assignment" that Citibank delivered "for value" "the Accounts listed in Exhibit 1 and final electronic file" (see Exhibit 1 attached).

A. Defendant translates the meaning of delivered "'for value' and 'the Accounts listed in Exhibit 1 and final electronic file'" to mean "the Plaintiff purchased any and all the pertinent records to prove Plaintiff's allegations on the alleged debt and has such evidence in Plaintiff's possession."

At least 6 courts have adopted an objective standard for "least sophisticated debtor." *Greco v. Trauner, Cohen & Thomas, L.L.P.,* 412 F.3d 360, 365-66 (2d Cir. 2005); *Wilson v. Quadramed Corp.,* 225 F.3d 350, 354-55 (3d Cir. 2000); *United States v. National Fin. Serv., Inc.,* 98 F.3d 131, 136 (4th Cir. 1996); *Smith v. Computer Credit, Inc.,* 167 F.3d 1052, 1054 (6th Cir. 1999); *Terran v. Kaplan,* 109 F.3d 1428, 1431-32 (9th Cir. 1997); *Jeter v. Credit Bureau, Inc.,* 760 F.2d 1168, 1174-75 (11th Cir.1985). The least sophisticated debtor test is "lower than simply examining whether particular language would deceive or mislead a reasonable debtor."

(1) On June 23, 2011, Plaintiff served on Defendant a "Notice of Production From Non-Party" that, outside of any objections from any party, a Subpoena Duces Tecum (Exhibit 4 attached) would be served on Citicorp Credit Services, Inc., USA, commanding to produce the card member agreement; checks; itemized statements reflecting purchases, payments, and financial charges; and signed application.

(2) During discovery, Plaintiff admits (Exhibit 5 attached) Plaintiff does not have these records/documents in their possession. This is a violation of Fl.R.Civ.P. Rule 1.130, as these records/documents were to be attached to the Complaint.

(3) Plaintiff also violated 15 U.S.C. § 1692e(2)(A) as it relates to Plaintiff's saying they are in possession of the "final electronic file": "A debt collector may not use any false, deceptive, or misleading representation or means in connection with the collection of any debt."

The fact that Plaintiff alleges in the "Bill of Sale and Assignment" (Exhibit 1) that Citibank delivered to Plaintiff "final electronic file" and then subpoenaing Citicorp Credit Services, Inc., for the same documentation is, at the least, false, deceptive and misleading.

B.  Plaintiff violated 15 U.S.C. § 1692e(2)(A) as it relates to the Card Agreement attached to the Plaintiff's Complaint: "A debt collector may not use any false, deceptive, or misleading representation or means in connection with the collection of any debt."

C.  In the Subpoena Duces Tecum, Plaintiff commands the Card Agreement be produced by Citicorp Credit Services, Inc., although Plaintiff attached an alleged Card Agreement to Plaintiff's Complaint, upon which Plaintiff based the Complaint. This constitutes a Sham Pleading by Fl.R.Civ.P. Rules 1.150.

D.  The Card Agreement (Exhibit 6 attached) that was attached to Plaintiff's Complaint displays a date of 2006 rather than 2004, the date Plaintiff alleges the alleged debt was initiated, which indicates it is false evidence on which the Complaint was based, further proven by the fact that Plaintiff issued a subpoena for the Card Agreement some 12 weeks later.

14.    Defendant filed a Counterclaim After Discovery on June 29, 2011.

A.  Plaintiff did not answer the Counterclaim within 20 days.

B.  The Defendant is entitled to a Default Summary Judgment in the matter.

173

15.    As a result of the acts by the Plaintiff, the Defendant has been irreparably damaged:

A.  The Plaintiff has a terminally ill daughter in her care, with a prognosis of 6-12 months to live (affidavit attached).

(1) Defendant revealed this to the Plaintiff during discovery.

(2) Emotional trauma experienced by the Defendant has inadvertently transmuted to Defendant's terminally ill daughter and, most probably, has shortened Defendant's daughter's life even further.

(3) As a result of her illness, Defendant's daughter experiences, as only part of her symptoms, severely high blood pressure and multiple life-threatening seizures, exacerbated by the understanding her mother is under a great amount of stress, as well as from the great decline in quantity and quality of time and care the Defendant has been able to provide while she is defending herself against a Sham Pleading.

(4) This has only deepened the emotional stress on the Defendant.

(5) Defending against this Sham Complaint has cost the Defendant precious hours in the last 4 months, away from Defendant's terminally ill daughter, precious time which can never be retrieved.

(6) Intentionally drawing the lawsuit out unnecessarily by not fully answering Interrogatories, not responding to a phone call and letter, and not setting hearings on filed motions has cost the Defendant precious hours away from Defendant's terminally ill daughter, precious time which can never be retrieved.

(7) Defendant was forced to impose on friends to find alternative methods of getting her daughter to medical care or finding others to sit with her while Defendant traveled to the Courthouse and/or post office, etc., printing and copying, research, etc., in defending herself against the Sham Complaint.

B.  Defendant has suffered personal stress symptoms of nausea, headaches, nervousness, embarrassment, sleeplessness, severe irritability, and marital stress, causing increased medical expenses.

C.  Defendant has had actual damages by incurring expenses for paper, supplies, printing expenses, and postage; travel expenses to and from Clerk of Court; hours of time away from family doing research/work; and loss of income.

## FIRST CLAIM FOR RELIEF – FDCPA VIOLATIONS

16.     Defendant repeats and re-alleges and incorporates by reference paragraphs 1 through 14.

A.  "The FDCPA is a strict liability statute, and one violation is sufficient to establish liability." *Bentley v. Great Lakes Coll. Bureau*, 6 F.3d 60 (2d Cir. 1993).

B.  The FDCPA was passed to eliminate abusive debt collection practices by debt collectors, to insure that those debt collectors who refrain from using abusive debt collection practices are not competitively disadvantaged, and to promote consistent State action to protect consumers against debt collection abuses. 15 U.S.C. § 1692.

C.  The Plaintiff violated 15 U.S.C. § 1692e(2)(A) by misrepresenting the character, amount, or legal status of any debt, by attempting to collect on an alleged debt when it was known by the Plaintiff that the Complaint filed was not precluded by a 30-day notice of the alleged Sale and Assignment of the debt.

D.  The Plaintiff violated 15 U.S.C. § 1692e(2)(A) by misrepresenting themselves as having in Plaintiff's possession the "final electronic file," upon which Plaintiff's Complaint was based.

E.  The Plaintiff violated 15 U.S.C. § 1692e(5) by filing an action on an alleged debt that is outside the Statute of Limitations by Delaware law.

F. Factors considered by Court, including, but not limited to, meeting deadlines stipulated by law:

15 U.S.C. § 1692k "In determining the amount of liability in any action under subsection (a) of this section, the courts shall consider, among other relevant factors –

(1) "in any individual action under subsection (a)(2)(A) of this section, the frequency and persistence of noncompliance by the debt collector, the nature of such noncompliance, and the extent to which such noncompliance was intentional;"

G. 15 U.S.C. § 1692k: "Any debt collector who fails to comply with any provision of this title with respect to any person is liable to such person in an amount equal to the sum of—

(1) any actual damage sustained by such person as a result of such failure;

(2) (A) in the case of any action by an individual, such additional damages as the court may allow, but not exceeding $1,000;

(3) in the case of any successful action to enforce the foregoing liability, the costs of the action, together with a reasonable attorney's fee as determined by the court."

17.    As a result of the above violations of the FDCPA, the Plaintiff is liable to the Defendant for declaratory judgment, actual damages, statutory damages, and attorney fees and costs.

## SECOND CLAIM FOR RELIEF – FLORIDA RULES OF CIVIL PROCEDURE VIOLATIONS

18.    Plaintiff repeats and re-alleges and incorporates by reference paragraphs 1-16.

19.    The Plaintiff violated the Florida Rules of Civil Procedure, including, but not limited to, the following:

A. The Plaintiff violated Fl.R.Civ.P. Rule 1.130 on no less than 3 counts, Attaching Copy of Cause of Action and Exhibits: "(a)

Instruments Attached. All bonds, notes, bills of exchange, contracts, accounts, or documents upon which action may be brought or defense made, or a copy thereof or a copy of the portions thereof material to the pleadings, shall be incorporated in or attached to the pleading. No papers shall be unnecessarily annexed as exhibits. The pleadings shall contain no unnecessary recitals of deeds, documents, contracts, or other instruments."

(1) Plaintiff did not attach the alleged Contract upon which "Breach of Contract" was based.

(2) Plaintiff did not attach the correct alleged Card Agreement upon which Plaintiff's Complaint was based, but rather is issuing a Subpoena Duces Tecum for it from Citicorp Credit Services, Inc.

(3) Plaintiff did not attach "Exhibit 1" specifying the account on which Plaintiff's Complaint was based and referenced in the alleged "Bill of Sale and Assignment."

20.    As a result of the above violations of the Florida Rules of Civil Procedure, the Plaintiff is liable to the Defendant for declaratory judgment, actual damages, statutory damages, and attorney fees and costs.

### THIRD CLAIM FOR RELIEF – FCCPA VIOLATIONS

21.    Plaintiff repeats and re-alleges and incorporates by reference paragraphs 1-19.

22.    The Plaintiff violated the FCCPA, including, but not limited to, the following:

A.  The Plaintiff violated FS § 559.715. Plaintiff failed to give Defendant written notice of assignment within 30 days.

B.  The Plaintiff violated FS § 559.72(9) on no less than 3 counts: In collecting consumer debts, no person shall "Claim, attempt, or threaten to enforce a debt when such persons know that the debt is not legitimate or assert the existence of some other legal right when such person knows that the right does not exist."

Plaintiff filed an action on alleged debt on which Plaintiff should have known they could not file,

       (1) Since their compliance with FS § 559.715 did not preclude the lawsuit;

       (2) Since the alleged debt was outside the Statute of Limitations by Delaware law; and

       (3) Since they did not have in their possession nor did they attach the copies of the documents upon which Plaintiff based the Complaints.

       C.  Plaintiff's acts, as described above, were done intentionally with the purpose of coercing the Defendant to pay an alleged debt.

       D.  As a result of the above violations of the FCCPA, the Plaintiff is liable to the Defendant for declaratory judgment, actual damages, statutory damages, punitive damages, and attorney fees and costs.

FCCPA § 559.72: "Upon adverse adjudication, the defendant shall be liable for actual damages and for additional statutory damages of up to $1,000, together with court costs and reasonable attorney's fees incurred by the plaintiff. In determining the defendant's liability for any additional statutory damages, the court shall consider the nature of the defendant's noncompliance with s.559.72, the frequency and persistence of such noncompliance, and the extent to which such noncompliance was intentional. . . . The court may, in its discretion, award punitive damages and may provide such equitable relief as it deems necessary or proper, including enjoining the defendant from further violations of this part."

WHEREFORE, Defendant respectfully prays that judgment be entered against the Plaintiff for the following:

A.     Default Summary Judgment with prejudice for the Defendant;

B.     Declaratory judgment and Actual and Statutory damages of $1,000 pursuant to FDCPA 15 USC § 1692k;

C.     Declaratory judgment and Actual damages/costs of $██████ pursuant to FCCPA § 559.72, calculated and running as follows:

Mileage to and from Court for filing $██████
8 x 20miles x  $██████
Postage $██████
Printing, copying, supplies $██████

D.     Declaratory judgment and Statutory damages of $1,000 pursuant to FCCPA §559.72;

E.     Additional Statutory damages of $1,000 per FCCPA violation (4 counts) pursuant to FCCPA § 559.72 (total of $4,000):

"In determining the defendant's liability for any additional statutory damages, the court shall consider the nature of the defendant's noncompliance with FCCPA § 559.72, the frequency and persistence of such noncompliance, and the extent to which such noncompliance was intentional."

F.     Award Defendant punitive damages and provide such equitable relief of $██████ pursuant to FCCPA § 559.72 for the quantity and quality of time lost in being with her terminally ill daughter in defending the lawsuit over the last four months. Not only did the Defendant need to vigorously defend herself in the lawsuit, but it was needlessly drawn out by the Plaintiff 's not responding in a timely manner to Discovery, Motions, and the Counterclaim;

G.     *Townsend v. Asset Acceptance Corp.*, No. 03-1921CI-88A (Fla. 6th Cir. App. Ct. August 6, 2004): "In addressing the issues involving damages, the Court finds that Section 559.77(2) specifically provides for three types of damages, in addition to court costs and reasonable attorney's fees. Those are actual damages, statutory damages up to $1,000, and punitive damages, which may be awarded in the trial court's discretion. In the Statement of Claim Townsend pled "damages as defined by Florida State Statute Section 559.77 **including but not limited to emotional distress and fear, embarrassment, damage to his reputation and**

**credit worthiness, economic damages and other damages.**" The Court finds that Townsend sufficiently pled all damages that were statutorily available, including actual and punitive damages. Indeed, as pointed out by Townsend, punitive damages can be award by the trial court "in its discretion" so that such a request for relief need not be express in the complaint." (emphasis added)

"Florida Statutes 768.73 Punitive damages; limitation.--
   (1)(a)  Except as provided in paragraphs (b) and (c), an award of punitive damages may not exceed the greater of:

   1. Three times the amount of compensatory damages awarded to each claimant entitled thereto, consistent with the remaining provisions of this section; or

   2. The sum of $500,000.

   (b)  Where the fact finder determines that the wrongful conduct proven under this section was motivated solely by unreasonable financial gain and determines that the unreasonably dangerous nature of the conduct, together with the high likelihood of injury resulting from the conduct, was actually known by the managing agent, director, officer, or other person responsible for making policy decisions on behalf of the defendant, it may award an amount of punitive damages not to exceed the greater of:

   1. Four times the amount of compensatory damages awarded to each claimant entitled thereto, consistent with the remaining provisions of this section; or

   2. The sum of $2 million.

   (c)  Where the fact finder determines that at the time of injury the defendant had a specific intent to harm the claimant and determines that the defendant's conduct did in fact harm the claimant, there shall be no cap on punitive damages."

H.     Award Defendant punitive damages and provide such equitable relief of $██████ pursuant to FCCPA § 559.72 for loss of income, personal stress symptoms of nausea, headaches, nervousness, embarrassment, sleeplessness, severe irritability, marital stress, and increased medical expenses;

I.     Plaintiff is to pay all court costs and attorney fee;

J.     For such other and further relief as the Court may find to be just and proper.

Dated the 26th day of July, 2011

_____

SHEILA R. MUNOZ, Defendant

## CERTIFICATE OF SERVICE

I hereby certify that a copy hereof has been furnished by First Class Mail to Plaintiff's employee/attorney this 29th day of June 2011, to the following address:

Amanda R. Duffy
Asset Acceptance, LLC
PO Box 9065
Brandon, FL 33509

_____

SHEILA R. MUNOZ, Defendant

August 12, 2011

VIA FACSIMILE ███

The Honorable ███
Polk County Courthouse
255 N Broadway
Bartow, FL 33830

**RE: Asset Acceptance LLC v Sheila R. Munoz, Case # 2011CC1415**

Dear Honorable ███

You are in receipt of a letter from Colleen Ashley on behalf of Attorney Amanda Duffy requesting the August 23, 2011, hearing in the above referenced case be rescheduled.

I object to having the hearing rescheduled.

I filed 3 Motions in May, 1 in June, and 2 in July. When no hearings were scheduled on the Motions, I called the Clerk's office, who transferred me to your office for direction, as I am pro se and was unsure how to proceed. Your JA, ███ was on vacation, so the person replacing her conferred with you and advised me to call and/or write Ms. Duffy to get hearings scheduled. Your replacement JA was kind enough to give me 4 dates in <u>early August</u> from which to choose.

I called and wrote (cc: The Honorable ███) to Ms. Duffy requesting she set hearings on the motions and gave her the 4 dates. There was no response.

Finally, you were kind enough to set the hearing.

I care for a terminally ill daughter. I already have replacement care in place for that morning for her. It would be an inconvenience to me and to the caregiver to reschedule the hearing.

All through this lawsuit Ms. Duffy has ignored timelines, ignored telephone calls, ignored letters. This hearing could have already transpired in early August had Ms. Duffy simply responded.

Therefore, I respectfully request that the hearing remain as scheduled. Thank you for your consideration.

Sincerely,

███

Sheila R. Munoz

Cc: Amanda Duffy, PO Box 9065, Brandon, FL 33509

# Chapter 6

## Asset Acceptance, LLC's, Motion To Strike Defendant's Counterclaim, Affidavit in Opposition to Defendant's Motion for Summary Judgment, and Voluntary Dismissal Without Prejudice

## Rework of My Counterclaim to Sue Asset Acceptance, LLC

*Note:* Asset Acceptance, LLC's, actual Motion To Strike Defendant's Counterclaim, Affidavit in Opposition to Defendant's Motion for Summary Judgment, and Notice of Voluntary Dismissal, as well as my reworked Counterclaim into a new lawsuit against Asset Acceptance, LLC, may be found at the end of this chapter.

Not all hearings will go as mine had. Judges are different; cases are different. This author can only share the actual experience of my defending myself pro se with the hopes that the reader can glean methods and tools to use in their own defense.

The judge ordered Amanda Duffy, Asset Acceptance, LLC's, in-house attorney, to write up an Order of the Court based on his findings and submit it to me. If both Amanda Duffy and I agreed that it represented what the judge ordered in court, he would sign it.

While waiting for the draft of the Court Order to arrive by mail, I ordered and looked over my credit reports. To my disdain, I discovered Asset Acceptance, LLC, had performed a pull of my credit report just a few days before the court hearing. Not only did Asset Acceptance, LLC, pull my credit, but they performed a hard pull rather than a soft pull that does not affect one's credit score. Of course, this would only drag down my already damaged credit score even more.

Not only did Asset Acceptance, LLC, pull my credit report, but it was done under false pretenses. Each time a company pulls one's credit, they have to give a certified reason for doing so. The FCRA gives specific reasons for pulling one's credit, and that reason has to be certified by the company pulling the credit. Any reason outside of those listed is considered an impermissible pull. If a company falsely gives the credit reporting agency a reason as to why they are pulling the credit, it is considered a pull under false pretenses and is punishable by jail time for up to two years.

Asset Acceptance, LLC's, reason for pulling my credit was "credit card." Even though the original debt was a credit card debt, once it was purchased by Asset Acceptance, LLC, it became a debt buyer debt. Asset Acceptance, LLC, has never offered me credit in any form, nor have I accepted credit from Asset Acceptance, LLC, in any form. This absolutely was a pull of my credit under false pretenses.

From my research, I knew a credit pull during litigation was illegal, a violation of FCRA 1681b(a)(3)(A) (*Pintos v. Pacific Creditors' Association*), as well as Asset Acceptance, LLC's, pull of my credit under false pretenses a criminal act. I had two more violations and damages to add to my new counterclaim I would be filing with the court in the near future.

I was hard at work on my new counterclaim, making sure to add the new FCRA violations. Almost a week had passed since the hearing. I went to my mailbox one day. In the stack of mail was a business envelope addressed to me. The return address was that of Asset Acceptance, LLC's, Brandon/Riverview office. "What now?" I thought.

Then I remembered I was expecting a draft of the judge's order. That had to be what it was. I ripped open the envelope. There was one sheet of paper: "Notice of Voluntary Dismissal." I had won!

Asset Acceptance, LLC, revealed later in a letter to the Florida Office of Financial Regulation in answer to a complaint I had filed against Asset Acceptance, LLC, that their reasoning for voluntary dismissal was the fact they had failed to give me notice within 30 days that they had purchased the debt. Of course, they violated a lot of other laws, also, that they did not own up to.

The Dismissal is stated "without prejudice." In theory, Asset Acceptance, LLC, could file another lawsuit on the same debt. But they would have to make corrections first. However, they could not correct that they had not given me notice of their acquisition of the debt within 30 days of that acquisition. Or they could sell the debt to another unsuspecting JDB, unsuspecting that the statute of limitations had run out on that debt.

Since the dismissal was voluntary by Asset of Acceptance, LLC, the statute of limitations, in effect, never stopped running during the lawsuit, and it had passed during the lawsuit. Of course, the negative tradeline would remain for seven years. And their illegal pull of my credit would remain for two years, affecting my credit score. This was not acceptable!

I decided to go ahead and file that lawsuit against Asset Acceptance, LLC, after all. I reworked my original counterclaim into a brand new lawsuit against Asset Acceptance, LLC, asking the court to grant statutory, actual, and punitive damages per Federal and state laws. In addition, I would demand Asset Acceptance, LLC, remove their tradeline and credit pull from my credit report.

Asset Acceptance, LLC, removed the case to Federal court. If a case is heard in Federal court, one must follow the Federal Rules of Civil Procedure. In addition, each Federal court district has its own local rules. These all can be found on the internet. Many judges also have personal preferences that must be followed. These can be found on the Federal court website for one's district. It is very important that one becomes familiar with these rules and follows them explicitly if their case is being heard in Federal court.

As a result, I had to amend (change) my Complaint to match Federal Rules of Civil Procedure.

Seven months later (one year and one week after Asset Acceptance, LLC, originally filed a lawsuit against me) Asset Acceptance, LLC, settled with me. Instead of getting a default judgment against me by not answering their Summons and Complaint, I beat them in their lawsuit against me. And now, after winning my lawsuit against Asset Acceptance, LLC, I have the debt expunged, tradeline removed, pull of credit report removed, and money in my pocket. And I did it all pro se! It can't get any better than that!

IN THE COUNTY COURT IN AND FOR POLK COUNTY, FLORIDA
CIVIL DIVISION

ASSET ACCEPTANCE LLC,
      Plaintiff,

vs.                            Case No: 2011 CC 1415

SHEILA R. MUNOZ,
      Defendant.
_____/

## PLAINTIFF'S MOTION TO STRIKE DEFENDANT'S COUNTERCLAIM

COMES NOW, Plaintiff, ASSET ACCEPTANCE LLC and files this Motion to Strike Defendant's Counterclaim After Discovery pursuant to Rule 1.170 and would state as follows:

1. Plaintiff filed their complaint for damages on or about March 21, 2011

2. Defendant filed an answer to Plaintiff's complaint on or about April 19, 2011. The answer is 4 single spaced pages long and Affirmative Defenses are pled. No Counterclaim was pled.

3. The allegations in defendant's Counterclaim are compulsory in character. As such, they were required to be pled in the answer or will be waived by the doctrine of res judicata.

4. Defendant counterclaim does not fall under any of the four exceptions recognized so as to permit a non-compulsory counterclaim.

5. The defendant has not sought leave of court or a stipulation by the parties to file an amended answer.

WHEREFORE the Plaintiff respectfully requests an order striking the Defendant's Counterclaim.

               ( ) Rodolfo J. Miro, Bar No.:0103799
               ( ) Anthony J. Steele, Bar No.:0074810
               ( ) Amanda R. Duffy, Bar No: 0035612
               Staff Attorneys for
               Asset Acceptance LLC
               P.O. Box 9065
               Brandon Fl. 33509
               (866) 266-7660 ext 2314

## CERTIFICATE OF SERVICE

**I HEREBY CERTIFY** that a true and correct copy of the forgoing was furnished by U.S. Mail to Sheila Munoz, ███████████████████████ on this ⌐9⌐ day of August, 2011.

               Amanda R. Duffy, Bar No: 0035612

# IN THE COUNTY COURT IN AND FOR POLK COUNTY, FLORIDA
## CIVIL DIVISION

ASSET ACCEPTANCE LLC,

    Plaintiff,

vs.                    Case No: 53 2011-CC-1415

SHEILA R. MUNOZ,

    Defendant.

_____/

## AFFIDAVIT IN OPPOSITION TO DEFENDANT'S MOTION FOR SUMMARY JUDGMENT

STATE OF FLORIDA        )
                         )
COUNTY OF HILLSBOROUGH  )

BEFORE ME, the undersigned authority appeared MICHELLE CRISTIANO-CUMMINS, who, after being duly sworn, deposes and says that:

1. I am the Legal Supervisor for Plaintiff, ASSET ACCEPTANCE LLC, in Hillsborough County, Florida. In preparing this Affidavit I have relied on my own personal knowledge as well as information contained in Asset Acceptance LLC's records. The events and items in the company's records are recorded at or near the time the events or items occurred. The records are kept in the course of regularly conducted business activity.

2. The records of the subject accounts are maintained under my supervision.

3. I have read the Defendant's Motion For Summary Judgment and in Defendant's claims for relief there aren't enough facts alleged for me to be able to determine if any of Defendant's claims are valid.

#10-400001837

4. There is a material fact as to the date of the assignment and date of the First Notice Letter.

5. I dispute that the court can grant the relief sought in Defendant's Sworn Denial, Motion to Strike Affidavit, Motion to Strike Card Agreement, and Motion to Strike Affidavit.

6. Defendant's alleged counter claim was not filed timely or appropriately and there was no leave of court granted.

7. Plaintiff's issuance of the Subpoena Duces Tecum to original creditor did not constitute any violation of state of federal law.

8. Plaintiff has not acted in any way to intentionally extend litigation unnecessarily.

9. There are several disputed facts at issue in this case and summary judgment is not appropriate.

FURTHER AFFIANT SAYETH NAUGHT.

_____
MICHELLE CRISTIANO-CUMMINS

SWORN AND SUBSCRIBED before me on this ___9___ day of ___August___,

2011 by MICHELLE CRISTIANO-CUMMINS, who is personally known to me.

_____
NOTARY PUBLIC, State of Florida

#10-400001837

## CERTIFICATE OF SERVICE

**I HEREBY CERTIFY** that a true and correct copy of the foregoing Affidavit In Opposition to Defendant's Motion For Summary Judgment was furnished by regular U.S. mail to Sheila R. Munoz, *Defendant,* ███████████████████████, this ___19___ day of August, 2011.

( ) Rodolfo J. Miro, Bar No.:0103799
( ) Anthony J. Steele, Bar No.:0074810
( ) Howard Butler, Bar No.: 0753041
(X) Amanda R. Duffy, Bar No: 0035612
Staff Attorneys for
Asset Acceptance LLC
P.O. Box 9065
Brandon FL 33509
(866) 266-7660; Ext 2387

#10-400001837

# IN THE COUNTY COURT IN AND FOR POLK COUNTY, FLORIDA
## CIVIL DIVISION

ASSET ACCEPTANCE LLC,

        Plaintiff,

vs.                            Case No.: 53 11-CC-1415

SHEILA R. MUNOZ,

        Defendant.

_____ /

## NOTICE OF VOLUNTARY DISMISSAL

COMES NOW, the Plaintiff, by and through its undersigned counsel and dismisses this action without prejudice pursuant to Fla. R. Civ. P. Rule 1.420 (a) (1).

_____
( ) Rodolfo J. Miro, Bar No. 0103799
( ) Anthony J. Steele, Bar No. 0074810
( ) Howard Butler, Bar No. 0753041
(X) Amanda Duffy, Bar No. 0035612
Staff Attorney for Plaintiff
ASSET ACCEPTANCE LLC
P.O. BOX 9065
BRANDON, FL 33509
(866) 266-7660
(813) 983-2519 facsimile

## CERTIFICATE OF SERVICE

**I HEREBY CERTIFY** that a true and correct copy of the foregoing Notice of Voluntary Dismissal was mailed to Sheila R. Munoz, *Defendant* at ▮▮▮▮▮▮▮▮ ▮▮▮▮ on this __31__ day of __August__ , 2011.

_____
( ) Rodolfo J. Miro, Bar No. 0103799
( ) Anthony J. Steele, Bar No. 0074810
( ) Howard Butler, Bar No. 0753041
(X) Amanda Duffy, Bar No. 0035612
Staff Attorney for Plaintiff
ASSET ACCEPTANCE LLC
P.O. BOX 9065
BRANDON, FL 33509
(866) 266-7660

# UNITED STATES DISTRICT COURT
## MIDDLE DISTRICT OF FLORIDA
### TAMPA DIVISION

SHEILA R. MUNOZ
     Plaintiff,

vs.

Case No. 8:11-cv-02247-MSS-TGW

ASSET ACCEPTANCE, LLC
     Defendant.

_____/

## AMENDED COMPLAINT AND JURY DEMAND

COMES NOW Plaintiff, Sheila R. Munoz, pro se, and brings this action against Defendant on the grounds set forth herein.

## PRELIMINARY STATEMENT

1.    Count I of Plaintiff's Complaint is based on the Florida Consumer Collections Practices Act (hereinafter FCCPA) Part IV of the Florida Statutes.

2.    Count II of Plaintiff's Complaint is based on the Fair Debt Collections Practices Act (hereinafter FDCPA) 15 U.S.C. § 1692 et seq.

3.    Count III of Plaintiff's Complaint is based on the Fair Credit Reporting Act (hereinafter FCRA) 15 U.S.C. § 1681 et seq.

4.    Count IV of Plaintiff's Complaint is based on Restatement of Torts, Second §652B.

## JURISDICTION AND VENUE

5.     Jurisdiction is conferred on this Court by 15 USC § 1692k(d), 28 USC § 1331 and 28 U.S.C. § 1367.

6.     Defendant conducts business in the state of Florida and, therefore, personal jurisdiction is established.

7.     Venue is proper pursuant to 28 USC 1391.

8.     Declaratory relief is available pursuant to 28 USC 2201 and 2202.

## PARTIES

9.     Plaintiff, a natural person, who resides in ██████████, Polk County, Florida.

10.    Plaintiff is a consumer as defined by 15 USC § 1692a(3), and according to Defendant Asset Acceptance, LLC (hereinafter AA), Plaintiff allegedly owes a consumer debt (alleged debt) as that term is defined by 15 USC 1692a(5), for personal, family, or household purposes.

11.    AA is a debt collector as defined by 15 USC § 1692a(6) and sought to collect an alleged consumer debt from Plaintiff.

12.    AA is a national company and conducts business throughout Florida.

13.    AA has been in the business of debt collection for approximately 50 years.

14.    AA has an ongoing training program for all account representatives on federal, state, and local collection laws with required

annual testing and minimum standard requirements of knowledge of these laws. Account representatives not achieving minimum standards are required to complete a review session and are then retested.

15.    There has never been a consumer relationship between Plaintiff and AA as there    has never been a consumer transaction between them involving the extension of credit, insurance, employment, or licensing.

16.    Defendant acted through its agents, employees, officers, members, directors, heirs, successors, assigns, principals, trustees, sureties, subrogees, representatives, and insurers.

## FACTUAL ALLEGATIONS

17.    F.S. 559.715 was amended during the 2010 Florida Legislative Session and went into effect October 1, 2010.

18.    Prior to October 1, 2010, F.S. 559.715 read:

"Assignment of consumer debts. This part does not prohibit the assignment, by a creditor, of the right to bill and collect a consumer debt. However, the assignee must give the debtor written notice of such assignment within 30 days after the assignment. The assignee is a real party in interest and may bring an action in a court of competent jurisdiction to collect a debt that has been assigned to such assignee and is in default."

19.    All Counts in this Complaint commenced and continued from Defendant's first communication with the Plaintiff in regard

to the alleged debt by letter dated August 9, 2010, and, therefore, is based on F.S. 559.715 as it read prior to October 1, 2010.

20.     Compliance with F.S. 559.715 is a condition precedent, without which precludes a debt collector the right to bill and collect a consumer debt.

21.     On June 29, 2010, Defendant was assigned or sold an alleged debt of the Plaintiff.

22.     On August 9, 2010, Defendant notified Plaintiff by letter of the assignment or purchase of the alleged debt, 42 days after the assignment or purchase.

23.     Since notification to Plaintiff of the assignment of the alleged debt was not accomplished by July 28, 2010, pursuant to F.S. 559.715, Defendant is precluded from the right to bill and to collect on the Plaintiff's alleged debt.

24.     The August 9, 2010, letter from AA states it is an "attempt to collect a debt."

25.     On August 20, 2010, AA account representative Jenna Wood called Plaintiff in an attempt to collect on the alleged debt.

26.     On September 27, 2010, AA account representative Scott Meyer called Plaintiff in an attempt to collect on the alleged debt.

27.     On October 6, 2010, AA account representative Scott Anderson called Plaintiff in an attempt to collect on the alleged debt.

28.     On November 26, 2010, AA account representative Jessica Felix called Plaintiff in an attempt to collect on the alleged debt.

29.     On March 17, 2011, AA account representative Denise Owens called Plaintiff in an attempt to collect on the alleged debt.

30.     On March 21, 2011, Amanda Duffy, as staff attorney for AA, filed a lawsuit against Plaintiff in County Civil Court in and for Polk County, Florida, in an attempt to collect on the alleged debt.

31.     On June 29, 2011, Plaintiff filed a Counterclaim to AA's lawsuit in which Plaintiff made aware to the Defendant of the alleged debt being unbillable and uncollectable by AA pursuant to F.S. 559.715.

32.     On July 25, 2011, Defendant performed a hard pull of Plaintiff's credit report.

33.     The certified reason Defendant gave for pulling the Plaintiff's credit report was "credit card."

34.     The Plaintiff does not have nor ever did have a credit card account with the Defendant. Once it was purchased by the Defendant, it became a "debt buyer account."

35.     The Defendant never extended an offer of credit to the Plaintiff.

36.     On August 31, 2011, the Defendant voluntarily dismissed their case against Plaintiff.

37.     On September 12, 2011, the Plaintiff transferred her Counterclaim in AA's lawsuit as a Complaint to the 10th Judicial Circuit Court in and for Polk County, Florida.

38.     The Complaint was subsequently removed to Federal Court by Defendant on October 4, 2011.

# CAUSES OF ACTION

## COUNT I

### FCCPA VIOLATION OF DEFENDANT AA

39.   Defendant violated FS 559.72(9) based on the following:

a.   Defendant willfully asserted a legal right that did not exist because the Plaintiff's alleged debt was precluded to be billable or collectable by AA after July 28, 2010.

b.   Defendant has in-depth knowledge of federal, state, and local debt collection laws through experience of approximately 50 years of being in the debt collection business; enforcing annual training and testing of all their employees on federal, state, and local laws; and the hiring of legal supervisors, compliance managers, and in-house attorneys.

c.   Defendant attempted to collect on Plaintiff's alleged debt through written and phone communication, as well as litigation, for over a year from August 9, 2010 - August 31, 2011.

d.   Plaintiff made Defendant aware that it was attempting to collect on an alleged debt that was precluded to be billable or collectable by AA.

## COUNT II

### FDCPA VIOLATIONS BY DEFENDANT AA

40.   Defendant AA violated the FDCPA based on the following:

a.   Defendant violated 15 USC § 1692e(2)(A) when it falsely represented the legal status of the Plaintiff's alleged debt in written and phone communications, as well as legal action, because Plaintiff's alleged debt was precluded to be billable or collectable by AA after July 28, 2010.

b. Defendant violated 15 USC § 1692e(5) when it threatened to take action that cannot legally be taken because Plaintiff's alleged debt was precluded to be billable or collectable by AA after July 28, 2010.

c. Defendant violated 15 USC § 1692e(8) when it communicated to credit reporting agencies negative credit information on the Plaintiff which was known or should have been known to be false because Plaintiff's alleged debt was precluded to be billable or collectable by AA after July 28, 2010.

d. Defendant violated 15 USC § 1692e(10) when it used false representation and deceptive means in written and phone communications and legal action to attempt to collect on Plaintiff's alleged debt because Plaintiff's alleged debt was precluded to be billable or collectable by AA after July 28, 2010.

e. Defendant violated 15 USC § 1692d by engaging in conduct the natural consequence of which was to harass, oppress, or abuse the Plaintiff by continuing to attempt to collect on the Plaintiff's alleged debt even after it was made aware by the Plaintiff the legal right to do so did not exist.

## COUNT III

## FCRA VIOLATIONS BY DEFENDANT AA

41.    Defendant AA violated the FCRA based on the following:

a. Defendant violated 15 USC 1681b by knowingly and willfully performing an impermissible hard pull of the Plaintiff's credit report on July 25, 2011.

b. A hard pull of one's credit harms one's credit score by dropping it lower.

c. Defendant knowingly and willfully obtained the Plaintiff's credit report under the false pretense of "credit card" while it was a "debt buyer account," which is a criminal act (15 USC 1681q).

d. Defendant knowingly and willfully has continued to report false information on the Plaintiff's alleged debt, even after the Plaintiff disputed the information with the credit reporting agency.

## COUNT IV

## VIOLATION OF RESTATEMENT OF TORTS,
## SECOND §652B BY AA

42.    Defendant violated Restatement of Torts, Second, §652B based on the following:

a.    Defendant attempted to collect on Plaintiff's alleged debt by phone and written communication, litigation, impermissible pull of Plaintiff's credit report, and reporting false information to credit reporting agencies, over a period of a year, August 9, 2010, to August 31, 2011.

b. Plaintiff's alleged debt was precluded to be billable or collectable by AA after July 28, 2010.

c. The Defendant's intrusion of Plaintiff's seclusion was highly offensive and would be highly offensive to any reasonable person.

d. The Defendant's intrusion of Plaintiff's seclusion was an invasion of privacy that caused great anguish and suffering and mental distress for Plaintiff as it prevented Plaintiff from caring for her terminally ill daughter to the degree Plaintiff and her daughter were accustomed prior to Defendant's actions while Plaintiff defended herself against Defendant's actions.

## CLAIMS FOR RELIEF

43. As a direct and proximate result of one or more or all of the statutory violations above, Plaintiff has suffered financial damage in actual expenses and lost income, anguish and suffering, mental and emotional distress, creditworthiness damage, invasion of privacy, and intrusion of seclusion.

## PRAYER FOR RELIEF

WHEREFORE, Plaintiff Sheila R. Munoz respectfully requests judgment be entered against Defendants for the following:

44. Declaratory judgment that the Defendant's conduct violated the FCCPA.

45. Declaratory judgment that the Defendant's conduct violated the FDCPA.

46. Declaratory judgment that the Defendant's conduct violated the FCRA.

47. Declaratory judgment that the Defendant's conduct violated Restatement of Torts, Second §652B.

48. Statutory damages pursuant to F.S. § 559.77(2), 15 USC § 1692k, 15 USC § 1681n and 15 USC §1681o.

49.	Actual damages.

50.	Costs.

51.	Damages and special damages pursuant to Restatement of Torts, Second, §652H.

52.	Any other relief that this Honorable Court deems appropriate.

## DEMAND FOR JURY TRIAL

Pursuant to Rule 38 of the Federal Rules of Civil Procedure, Plaintiff respectfully demands trial by jury in this issue of all issues so triable.

Dated this 13th day of February, 2012.

Respectfully Submitted

SHEILA R. MUNOZ, Plaintiff

## CERTIFICATE OF SERVICE

UNDER PENALTY OF PERJURY, PLAINTIFF Sheila R. Munoz hereby certifies that she furnished a copy of the forgoing by First Class mail to opposing counsel on behalf of Defendant this 13th day of February, 2012:

Kenneth C. Grace

Dayle M. Van Hoose

Sessions, Fishman, Nathan & Israel, LLC

3350 Buschwood Park Dr., Ste. 195

Tampa, FL 33618

SHEILA R. MUNOZ, Plaintiff

# Chapter 7

# Filing Complaints to Regulators

*Note:* Most complaints can be *filed online* to different regulators. The website links to the regulators to whom I complained about Asset Acceptance, LLC's, actions may be found at the end of this chapter.

It is this author's opinion that filing of complaints to regulators who oversee debt collectors and their attorneys is extremely important. These complaints will, most likely, not result in helping one's case; however, collectively, over time, when different regulators receive hundreds or even thousands of letters from consumers, complaining of the same abuse by the same company, they finally are moved to look into it.

It is important to use proper grammar, punctuation, and spelling when filling out these forms or when writing an actual letter. To be taken seriously, the complaint must be in a professional tone: simply stating the laws that were violated, such as the FDCPA, FCRA, and others, and how the collection agency violated those laws. The complaint should be straight to the point without emotion. Most regulators will want documentation, if any, as evidence of the collection agency's violations.

In January, 2012, Asset Acceptance, LLC, was fined $2.5 million by the FTC (Federal Trade Commission) in response to thousands of complaints from consumers for Asset Acceptance, LLC's, abusive debt collection tactics and infractions of the law. That may seem like a lot of money. However, on Asset Acceptance, LLC's, website, one may see that their annual income is approximately $250 million. This fine was only 1% of their annual income. To put that in perspective, it would be the same if a person having an annual income of $35,000 was given a moving violation ticket of approximately $350.

That fine was a small slap on the hand to Asset Acceptance, LLC. But even fines such as that will most likely never materialize if consumers such as you and me do not take a stand and speak out! It takes moments to send off a letter or fill out an online complaint. It may help another consumer on down the road by helping to enforce the law or slapping more and bigger fines on abusive debt collectors.

Do I believe debt collection companies be outlawed? No. I believe in capitalism. However, I do believe they need to comply with the law. I do not necessarily believe we need more laws against debt collectors. I DO believe the laws we have need to be unequivocally enforced! And I believe the punishment for infractions need to be greater: greater fines, closing down debt collection companies who refuse to comply with the law, and even jail time.

On the website for Asset Acceptance, LLC, there is a Press Release dated July 28, 2010, in which Asset Acceptance, LLC, states that one of the things that may impair their ability to earn what they project to earn is, ". . . a decrease in collections if changes in or **enforcement of** debt collection laws impair our ability to collect." (emphasis added)

This statement indicates the attitude of Asset Acceptance, LLC, toward their compliance of the law. Rather than having an attitude of compliance, it is an attitude of not getting caught. Their words indicate a concern about <u>enforcement</u> of the law; not <u>compliance</u> with the law.

As consumers, when we encounter abusive debt collection practices, it is in our best interest and the interest of fellow consumers to stand and fight, as well as make regulators aware of our individual fight. Take the time to file complaints.

Most complaints may be filed online:

**Federal Trade Commission (FTC)**
www.ftc.gov

**Florida Bar Association**
www.floridabar.org
Under "Public/Consumers" is a link to the online complaint form.

**Florida Office of the Attorney General**
www.myfloridalegal.com
Link "File a Complaint"

**Delaware Office of the Attorney General**
(Asset Acceptance, LLC, is a Delaware corporation.)
**www.attorneygeneral.delaware.gov/consumers/
protection/complaint.shtml**

**Florida Office of Financial Regulation**
www.flofr.com
Under "Consumers" is a link, "File a Complaint."

**Better Business Bureau**
www.bbb.org/file-a-complaint
A complaint may be filed for the headquarters, as well as for
the office located on one's state, if applicable.

**Michigan Department of Licensing and Regulatory Affairs**
(Asset Acceptance, LLC's headquarters is in Michigan.)
**www.michigan.gov/lara**
The complaint form is under Commercial Services>
Consumer Services & Enforcement>Forms & Services>
Statement of Complaint

**Michigan Office of the Attorney General**
www.michigan.gov/ag/
Find the link under "Online Services>Consumer Complaint/Inquiry
Filing Information."

If you enjoyed this book,
I would be extremely grateful if you would leave
a brief review on Amazon at:

https://www.amazon.com/Defending-Lawsuit-Buyer-Collection-Agency/dp/1475214960

To connect with Sheila:
sheilaraeboyd@gmail.com
https://www.facebook.com/sheilaraeboyd/